Stratification Among the Aged

BROOKS/COLE SERIES IN SOCIAL GERONTOLOGY

Vern Bengtson, *University of Southern California*
Series Editor

HEALTH AND AGING
Tom Hickey, *University of Michigan*

ENVIRONMENT AND AGING
M. Powell Lawton, *Philadelphia Geriatric Center*

LAST CHAPTERS: A SOCIOLOGY OF AGING AND DYING
Victor W. Marshall, *University of Toronto and McMaster University*

AGING AND RETIREMENT
Anne Foner, *Rutgers University*
Karen Schwab, *Social Security Administration, Washington, D.C.*

ROLE TRANSITIONS IN LATER LIFE
Linda K. George, *Duke University Medical Center*

STRATIFICATION AMONG THE AGED
James J. Dowd, *University of Georgia*

Stratification Among the Aged

James J. Dowd
University of Georgia

Brooks/Cole Publishing Company
Monterey, California
A Division of Wadsworth, Inc.

Printed in the United States of America

10 9 8 7 6 5 4 3 2 1

Library of Congress Cataloging in Publication Data

Dowd, James J
    Stratification among the aged.

    (Brooks/Cole series in social gerontology)
    Bibliography: p. 133
    Includes index.
    1. Gerontology. 2. Social classes. 3. Social status. 4. Power (Social sciences) I. Title.
II. Series.
HQ1061.D67   301.43'5   79-25143
ISBN 0-8185-0386-6

Acquisition Editor: *Todd Lueders*
Production Editor: *Stacey C. Sawyer*
Series Design: *John Edeen*
Illustrations: *Ayxa Art*
Typesetting: *Graphic Typesetting Service*

For my parents,
Margaret M. Dowd
and Patrick M. Dowd (1905–1957)

Foreword

Aging may be inherently problematic, but the difficulties of old age certainly are not evenly distributed. What is it that makes growing old less difficult for some people or groups than for others? Why is aging so often viewed negatively in our culture?

Most current answers to such questions are couched in psychological or physiological terms, drawing on observable individual differences in function or competence. In this book, however, a radically sociological explanation is suggested. As manifest in the day-to-day social encounters that make up human interaction, *aging is social exchange,* a continuous and delicate negotiation between individuals or groups who have different amounts of relative social power in a variously stratified social system.

Dr. James Dowd, Assistant Professor of Sociology at the University of Georgia, marshals both classical social theories and contemporary research data in support of his thesis: the greater the relative power of the individual older person, the greater the likelihood he or she will be able to negotiate a favorable outcome. The "Social Problem" of aging is that the elderly possess, relative to other age groups, lower status in the sense of negotiable power, privilege, and prestige; they are in an unfavorable exchange position. To understand either the process of aging or life in old age, it is necessary to explicate the relationship between age and the possession of resources, stratification, and the mechanisms of exchange.

Dr. Dowd's analysis of social structure and aging does not paint a rosy portrait of eldership in contemporary Western society. Nor is his assessment of past "theory" in social gerontology flattering. Dr. Dowd points to its reluctance to draw directly from older, more traditional statements of *social* theory and its reluctance to admit its own social origins (and bias).

Basic to his approach to social gerontology is comparative analysis: contrasting the aged with the young, comparing the elderly poor to the wealthy aged, examining aging in traditional or "emergent" societies in contrast to growing old in industrialized, Western cultures, comparing the elderly in age-homogeneous settings (such as retirement communities) with those in age-heterogeneous environs (traditional suburban living). The comparative approach is, of course, basic to sociological inquiry. Unfortunately, as Dr. Dowd notes, it rarely has been rigorously pursued in the three decades since social gerontology first emerged as a recognizable (if low-status) scientific specialty. Thus the data are frequently insufficient to make adequate comparative statements. But from Dr. Dowd's exhaustive literature review one sees the nexus of a truly *social* gerontology, based on analyses of social structure informed by observations at both micro- and macro-social levels.

This volume is one of a series in social gerontology presented by Brooks/Cole Publishing Company. The books in this series review the state of the art in the growing scientific specialty of gerontology. Topics include health and aging, role transitions and stress in aging, sociological aspects of death and dying, retirement, and environment and aging.

Several themes that emerged in the last decade are central to a more informed social gerontology and serve as the foundation for the Brooks/Cole Series. They are aptly illustrated in Dr. Dowd's presentation of stratification and aging. The first concerns the *interplay between basic and applied knowledge* in social gerontology. Nothing is quite so practical as a good theory; Dowd's call for explicit and concise model building reflects the current urgent need for policy-relevant research on aging.

A second theme is the *necessity of both micro- and macro-level analysis* of phenomena related to aging. Dr. Dowd's treatment of aging as exchange exemplifies the advantages of macrosocial and microsocial theory building, while also illustrating the complexity that has made such dual-level analysis rare.

Third is the importance of *continuity as a framework as well as change*. Decrement and loss are the stereotypic consequences of changes associated with aging; but these must be considered along with the continuities of past coping behavior and competence—as well as the new opportunities of freedom and change brought by seniorhood. Dr. Dowd notes some exchanges in which old people hold frequently overlooked resources that can be translated into social power.

A fourth theme involves explicit *comparative analysis,* a comparison of aging in various social settings. Old age varies by historical and cultural context; and, as Dr. Dowd observes, the population of today's aged is considerably diverse, requiring comparison between social groups—defined by social class, ethnicity, race—instead of the mistaken assumption that all old people are alike.

This is an exciting book, one of the most intriguing that has come across my desk in recent years. It will also be a controversial book; many readers will not like what they find here. This is, in fact, precisely the author's intent: to provoke useful controversy in gerontological analysis.

Vern L. Bengtson
Series Editor

Preface

Sociologists in many societies are focusing their research on the problems of the aged. This text summarizes many theories in social gerontology and examines the problems of the aged from a new perspective: the relationship of stratification and aging. In other words, I focus on the relationship of the process of aging to the social-class membership of the aged person. We grow old differently, and an important factor that determines *how* we age is the degree of control we have in our daily lives over events and people. Usually our degree of control is in direct proportion to our social class and our rankings on other measures of status. Thus, to understand the situation of aged people in any society, we must examine the relationship of the society's stratification system to the aging process.

Although this text is written primarily for social gerontology and sociology students, I believe that professionals in these fields will find useful material in it. It presents a comprehensive examination of the aging process that is based on an understanding of the distribution of power resources among age groups.

The text is organized around the following three themes: (1) The ability of different age groups to obtain desirable interaction outcomes has structural bases in the society's political economy and system of social stratification; (2) On the individual level, diffuse status characteristics are translated into power resources that are used by aged people in everyday social encounters; (3) Talk and other forms of conversation are the mechanisms by which power resources, including status characteristics, are activated and used in social interaction.

The text is divided into seven chapters, beginning with a discussion of contemporary paradigms and perspectives within the field of social gerontology and ending, in Chapter 7, with an overview of social-policy considerations based on the relationship between aging and social class. In Chapters 2 and 3,

I present a view of aging and old age that is based largely on two frequently divergent points of view within sociology—exchange theory and symbolic interactionism. From this perspective, aging is viewed essentially as a process of negotiation, or exchange, among social "actors."

Chapters 4 and 5 discuss the historical, demographic, and economic factors that have produced the devaluation of old age. The social-psychological implications of a devalued status for old age are the subject of Chapter 6.

In several places in the text I present arguments that are critical of the ideas of other social gerontologists. Rather than emphasize the many points of agreement between us, I have chosen to stress the points on which we disagree. However, my criticisms of these materials are not meant to detract from their overall merit or to suggest that I did not find them helpful. Also, because of the complexity of the issues I am dealing with, the arguments presented in the book are not intended to be definitive, but, rather, they are intended to be identifications of problems for discussion. Readers who are unfamiliar with some of the terms used in the discussion will find the glossary of terms at the end of the text helpful.

In closing, I would like to acknowledge the following individuals for their help in the completion of this book: Vern L. Bengtson, my friend, colleague, and teacher, for enthusiasm and encouragement from the beginning of the project; Leonard D. Cain, Portland State University, Vincent Jeffries, California State University at Northridge, and Harold Orbach, Kansas State University, for their reviews of the original manuscript. For their patience, I thank my wife Laura, and my children, Aimee, Christopher, and Emily. For her preparation of the manuscript for publication, I thank Stacey Sawyer.

James J. Dowd

Contents

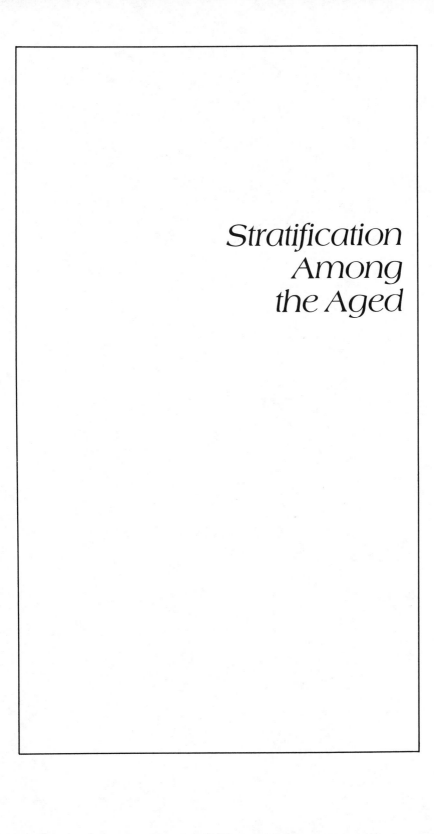

*Stratification
Among
the Aged*

1

Old
People
and
Sociological
Analysis

Introduction

The prevailing political economy of Western industrialized societies is an advanced, or monopolistic, form of **capitalism**. **Monopolistic capitalism** is an economic system characterized by a core industrial sector that is dominated by a few large corporate enterprises. (Baran & Sweezy, 1966). In the United States, this advanced form of capitalism is the result of a century and a half of economic change during which the ownership of property became increasingly concentrated. During the early phase of capitalism in the United States—the phase called *competitive capitalism*—and particularly during the early part of the 19th century, the ownership of property was much more diffused. Some economists have estimated that, excluding slaves, approximately 80% of the working population "owned the means of production with which they worked" (Bottomore, 1968, p. 48). During this period the United States was, as Bottomore notes, a nation of small farmers, small traders, and small businessmen. The transition from the competitive to the monopolistic form of capitalism in the United States started in the railroad industry around 1875 and continued in the steel, coal, and textile industries between 1900 and 1920 (Reich, Gordon, & Edwards, 1977).

The status of old people living in a monopolistic-capitalistic economy is considerably different from the status of old people living in societies characterized by an **agrarian** economy. Although in both economies the old person's life-style is determined by social-class membership, resources are distributed differently in each economy to members of different age groups within the same **social class.** The primary focus of the discussion that follows is on modern Western societies, although relevant aspects of other societies, past and present, will also be analyzed. The discussion has two goals: first, the investigation of the effects on the individual old person of the unequal distribution of society's resources to different social classes; and, second, the identification of the mechanisms by which resources, once acquired, become part of the daily routine of social life—in other words, how inequality of **status,** wealth, and prestige become manifest in social interaction. The guiding principle underlying this discussion is that, possession of—or lack of —resources largely determines everyday social life. Therefore, to understand either the process of human aging or life in old age, it is essential that we become aware of the relationship between age and the possession and utilization of resources.

The Movement of Ideas in Social Science

Of course, there are two sides to almost everything, including scientific theory. For example, sociology in the United States has been characterized by a methodological dualism for at least 50 years. Factions supporting either **quantitative**[1] or **qualitative methodology** persist within the discipline, and successive generations of sociologists continue to reargue the early debates between Herbert Blumer and George Lundberg concerning the nature of **operational definitions.** Similarly, the reoccurring doubts concerning the utility of **micro-** and **macro-level analyses** provide another example of this duality. **Social gerontology,** despite its relatively brief existence as a scientific discipline, has shown a similar tendency towards factionalism. For example, the classic study of aging in the Midwest, *Growing old: A process of disengagement* (Cumming & Henry, 1961), was the impetus behind the development of **activity theory,** which contradicted the point of view presented in the study.

The fact that there are conflicting opinions within the realm of science on the origins and the causes of phenomena is neither newsworthy nor much

---

[1] Terms that appear in **boldface** are explained in the Glossary at the back of the book.

of a problem. In fact, not only would social intercourse become unbearably routine if everyone agreed with one another, but, without the dynamic process of idea development produced by a confrontation of opposing views, science would advance in understanding slowly, if at all. And, if we neglect debate and argument in science, we run the risk of allowing a particular explanation to enter our consciousness as something essential—a truth that is "scientifically" supported and is, therefore, one to be taken for granted. Fortunately, scientific truth is rarely established without debate, because proponents of competing views are always ready to challenge each other's position.

The basic dialectic that underlies progress in science is perpetuated by several factors, including peer recognition and other job-related rewards given to those who participate in scientific debate. Another factor that encourages dialogue and decreases the probability of a single, unified view emerging in the social sciences is the interesting association between **ideology** and social class: ideas do not emerge from nothing but are grounded in the social backgrounds of their creators.[2] Thus, for example, the perspective of the **stratification** theorist is strongly influenced by the theorist's own social-class identity. Furthermore, this perspective in all likelihood favors the interests of the social class (or racial/ethnic group or age **stratum**) to which the theorist belongs. In light of this, it is not surprising that scientists view the same world differently and develop differing theoretical accounts of what they see. However, it is essential to the process of "doing" science that the social nature of the prevailing scientific **theories** be recognized. Thus, we must keep in mind that the ideas and theories existing within the intersecting disciplines discussed in this text—social stratification and social gerontology—reflect the social background of their originators.

A major difference between stratification and gerontology is that the stratification debate is, at least in part, recognized as ideological, whereas the gerontology debate (which is minimal) is not. For example, within the sphere of stratification, the continuing dialogue between the proponents of **functionalist** and neo-Marxist views on social mobility is generally recognized as a clash of ideologies—one ideology representing a middle-class understanding of reality and the other a working-class perception. The dominance of functionalist **role theory** in gerontology, however, remains unchallenged, and, although this is due in large part to the lack of theoretical training among gerontologists and the "applied" focus of aging-related funding agencies, the net result of the dominance of this theory is a lack of recognition of the middle-class bias of

---

[2] A brilliant essay on this subject was written several decades ago by Hans Speier (1938) and has since been updated by social phenomenologists such as Peter Berger. From the phenomenological perspective, all reality (including ideas and personal Weltanschauung) is socially constructed. For an insightful analysis of the social origins of the foremost American sociologist of this century, Talcott Parsons—an analysis that has produced considerable controversy—see Gouldner (1970). A less acrimonious account, in which the writer traces his own influential ideas to his upper-class Bostonian background, can be found in the autobiographical introduction to Homans (1962).

---

social gerontology. The next two sections of this chapter will discuss in more detail some of the competing theories and perspectives of gerontology and stratification.

Theories of Social Gerontology

Since its development during the years immediately following World War II, social gerontology (the study of the social aspects of aging) has been characterized by a lack of concern with conceptualization or theory-building. In this case, *theory* is not used in the restrictive sense—that is, meaning a set of interrelated principles and definitions from which a series of logically connected, empirically verifiable propositions are derived. (Social gerontology is not alone among the academic disciplines in its indifference to theorizing of this sort.) Rather, social gerontology's lack of concern with theory-building means that the published work of social gerontologists often displays a noticeable disinclination to test, generate, or formulate explicit, basic theoretical statements. Conceptualization, rather than the statement of relationships among propositions, is the essential meaning of the term *theory* as it is used here. It may be no more than a concept or a heuristic phrase that, when applied to the phenomenon under investigation, permits insight or a fresh perspective.

Although social gerontologists may not present research findings in a theoretical style, however, they do use a theoretical model of the aging process in their work. Social gerontology is, in fact, "theory-laden." The point is, however, that the components of the model of the aging process—the tacit framework of social gerontology—rarely, if ever, enter the research process as explicit and testable theory. The model remains in the background as an analogue of reality that suggests to the researcher what words to use in describing observations. A problem arises from the presumption that one researcher's particular perception of the reality of human aging is shared by others. Given the diversity of human experience, it is impossible for all social gerontologists to share a single view or understanding of aging.

Structural Functionalism

For over two decades the development of gerontology has been influenced primarily by a functionalist model of **social structure** and human development; this model sometimes appears as a form of "role theory" (for example, Cottrell, 1942; Phillips, 1957). However, the guiding assumptions of the unspoken ideology of functionalism (which includes, most notably, the view that old age in contemporary society is inherently stressful because of the lack of viable roles for old people and the absence of the normative "blueprints" or "scripts" associated with the roles) are rarely, if ever, subjected to close scrutiny.

The dominance of the **structural-functionalist perspective** within sociology, from the decline of the Chicago "School" in the 1930s to the emergence of "new" sociologies during the 1960s[3] is reflected in the approach sociologists initially took to the study of aging. Both of the two most important social-gerontological monographs published during the 1940s placed a major emphasis on the nature of individual adjustment to role change in old age.[4] Pollak notes, for example, that problems in old age arise either from declining physical and mental capacities *or* from "changes in social role and status assignments" (1948, p. 40.).

The functionalist orientation can be seen as well in the tendency of the pioneers in social gerontology to conceptualize age-related difficulties as problems of individual adjustment rather than as evidence of society's structural flaws. One example of this concerns role changes like those caused by enforced retirement. In this case, Pollak notes that the "individual who is able to make these changes quickly and effectively adjusts well to his problems of aging. The individual who cannot do so becomes the socially ineffective and unhappy old person whose problems challenge the research worker to determine their causes and their solution" (1948, p. 40).

Basing his work on an analysis of similar conceptions of age-related difficulties underlying prevailing theoretical paradigms, the British sociologist, Dawe, identified *two* distinct approaches to sociology: the **normative** and the **interpretive** approach (1970). These two opposing ideologies appear not only in the writings of sociological theorists, but they also pervade the empirical research (and the social policies that draw upon this research) of social gerontologists.[5]

The Normative Perspective

The *normative perspective* (in the guise of structural-functionalism) is, and has been for decades, the dominant view in American sociology. This perspective emphasizes the critical importance of social control, or order, in the conduct of human affairs. As Dawe wrote, the essence of this view "is that, since individuals cannot of their own volition create and maintain order, constraint is necessary for society to exist at all" (Dawe, 1970, p. 208). The principal means of insuring a stable social order is through socialization, the

---

[3] Although the emergence of functionalism in the 1930s coincided with the decline of the Chicago school, the former cannot be said to have caused the latter. The shift of the sociological "center" in the 1930s from Chicago to Harvard was due in part to the deaths or retirement of such dominant figures as Robert Park, George Herbert Mead, and John Dewey and, in part, to the "arrival" of Talcott Parsons as a major figure in sociological theory. Parsons' reputation was established with such important works as *The Structure of Social Action* (1937) and *The Social System* (1951).

[4] I refer here to Pollak's *Social Adjustment in Old Age* (1948) and Cavan, Burgess, Havighurst, and Goldhammer's *Personal Adjustment in Old Age* (1949).

[5] This particular point has been argued recently by Marshall (1979).

---

mechanism that links normative expectations with particular social statuses. Social control or normative constraint becomes "total through internalization." The mysteries of social order and everyday social behavior are thus solved: societies persist and behavior is controlled through the internalization of shared norms.

The Interpretive Perspective

The *interpretive perspective,* in contrast, does not view social order as its major theoretical concern. Although, according to Dawe, it does share common roots with the normative position in the Enlightenment, this "sociology" is concerned more with the "problems of control"—that is, "how human beings could regain individual *control* over essentially man-made institutions and historical situations" (Dawe, 1970, p. 211). This concern led, perhaps inevitably, to a view of individual social action as less controlled by social institutions and external norms than individual social action as viewed by normative sociologists. The interpretive position is evident in the optimistic vision of the future contained in the pragmatism of James and Dewey and the interactionism of Mead, Park, and W. I. Thomas. (The interactionist position assumes that people are social actors who define and, thereby, control their own situations.)[6]

Interpretive sociology emphasizes the fact that social structures come into being and are maintained by a continuous process of human interaction. Although social institutions constantly exercise varying degrees of control over individual behavior, the institutions themselves are subject to change, because the socialization of new "recruits" involves bilateral negotiation (Bengtson & Black, 1973). The individual must negotiate with pre-existing social organizations, but, in so doing, both the individual and the structure are transformed. In the interpretive view, society is seen not as a thing in itself but as a collection of individuals in social interaction.

At this point, even the patient reader may question how a discussion of contrasting metatheoretical assumptions relates to a study of stratification processes in old age. The answer is that past and current research in both aging and stratification reflects to a certain degree the effects of the ideological conflict between the normative and interpretive perspectives.

The Disengagement/Activity Paradigm

Earlier in the chapter we noted that the development of social gerontology has been influenced primarily by a functionalist model of social structure and human development. The disengagement/activity paradigm, which is

[6]For an excellent analysis of the origins of interactionism within the Chicago school, see Fisher and Strauss (1978).

steeped in functionalist role theory and which is, therefore, in the normative mode, has been a dominant form of functionalism during that development.

Although gerontologists frequently view the **disengagement** and activity theories as competing perspectives, the theories actually have much in common. Neither theory, for example, acknowledges the possibility of a variable social structure; that is, by phrasing its explanations of aging in terms of the individual, each theory underemphasizes the role of social structure on human behavior. (The social organization of modern societies is quite different from that of traditional societies and individual behavior varies across different societies as a function of the level of societal and economic complexity.) Disengagement theory posits the social withdrawal of old people as a universal cultural process that occurs regardless of social-structure variation among societies. In activity theory, social structure is acknowledged only to the extent that income (and, presumably, social class) influences the length of time an aging individual is able to retain a greater number of social roles; for example, a high income permits an old person to retain social roles for a longer-than-average length of time. The correlation between "successful aging" and social class was apparently either unrecognized or considered irrelevant to the theory. In any case, the structural implications of activity theory remain undeveloped.

Another point that the two theories have in common is their lack of understanding of the degree to which individuals, although they are products of social forces, are also autonomous agents in the continuous creation of social order and reality. The individual is, in other words, both an independent and a dependent variable (see Figure 1-1). Yet, the disengagement/activity paradigm overlooks the *autonomy* of aged social actors and sees only people who are either captives of their awareness of their mortality or script-reading occupants of social roles. The influence that the individual has on society through the formation of social agreements and understandings—by using cooperation, negotiation, force, duplicity, or any other means—is disregarded by activity and disengagement theorists.

Both activity and disengagement theories also assume that social interaction decreases in old age. Neither theory, however, attempts to offer more than a perfunctory explanation for the decreased social interaction or engagement, that occurs in old age. The reasons for this universal decline in interaction are too apparent, presumably, to warrant extended consideration by many theorists. These reasons include, for example, the fact that old people have lower incomes and poorer health than younger people, and, consequently, they are often physically and financially unable to remain as engaged in social roles and life as they once were. The death of a spouse is another event that, especially for older women, reduces social interaction. However, neither theory considers whether the decreased interaction that comes with aging could actually be caused by something other than obvious biologically related losses. This is a point that I have made elsewhere (1975) and that I will develop later in the text.

SOCIETY ————————⟶ INDIVIDUALS ——————————⟶ SOCIETY

FIGURE 1-1.   Individuals: Subjects and objects

A final point the two gerontological theories, activity and disengagement, have in common is their grounding in sociological functionalism.[7] Functionalist theorists attempt to understand and explain social phenomena in terms of the functions these social phenomena serve in the maintenance of society. Functionalists also tend to ascribe to functional structures the status of sine qua non; that is to say, structures that serve a function in a society must therefore be necessary for the society's continued existence. Both disengagement and activity theories use similar logic but different structures as their "functional requisites"—that is, those aspects of social organization that are necessary for the society's survival, such as a stable system of distributing the economic surplus. On the one hand, disengagement theory posits the functional necessity of both the exclusion of the aged individual by society and the withdrawal of the aging individual from society in order to insure both smooth **cohort** flow[8] as well as individual tranquility prior to death. Activity theory, by contrast, views the maintenance of social roles as the source of the aged individual's well-being. Since the number and functional importance of individually held roles generally peak in middle-age and then decline steadily with increasing age, the problem of aging is essentially a loss of functional roles. Without roles to perform, the essence of functional behavior is lost.

One may question at this point whether I am overstating the theoretical problems of social gerontology. After all, assuming that the perspective offered by the disengagement/activity paradigm, complete with its functionalist role-theory undertones, is legitimate and, perhaps, even illuminating, wherein lies the problem? The basis of the problem lies in the nature of the social and behavioral sciences. Unlike the sciences of quantum physics and plate tectonics, which are characterized by highly developed paradigms, the human sciences are multi-paradigm in nature; that is, human behavior, which is the subject matter of sociology or social gerontology, is too broad and complex to be explained by a single theoretical framework. The alternation between (or even the simultaneous occurrence of) cooperation and conflict

[7]Specific differences between the two theories involve their different predictions of the effect of declining social interaction on morale and their different views on whether the withdrawal of the aged from society is voluntary or mandated by the requirement that societies, in order to survive, must develop mechanisms of replacing older role incumbents with younger ones. Empirical evidence generally supports the critics of disengagement theory who had difficulty accepting the possibility that disengagement in old age was voluntary and could ever result in a psychological equilibrium marked by high morale. However, the differences between the theories are relatively insignificant when they are compared to the points the theories have in common.

[8]The term *cohort flow* refers to the rhythm of birth and death; old people die and are replaced by younger people.

within a single group produces dual theories. As mentioned earlier, the fact that most phenomena have at least two sides (historical epochs, for example, can be characterized by both war *and* peace, turbulence *and* stability, or growth *and* decline) suggests the necessity of developing several theories in order to manage this diversity.

In consequence, even if one were satisfied that the disengagement/activity paradigm aided in explaining an observed pattern, the explanation would probably be incomplete. This is the case with social gerontology today; the explanations that it offers are incomplete. The normative side of social behavior has been emphasized without any parallel development of an interpretive view of behavior in old age. For more than three decades, gerontological research has reinforced the image of old age as a "roleless role" and a period of time in which feelings of marginality and uselessness are likely to occur, due to the lessening of normative constraints (cf. Cavan et al., 1949; Cottrell, 1942). The antidote to these miseries has been part of our folk wisdom for centuries and part of gerontological wisdom at least since the early 1950s; that is, remain active in old age and make creative use of leisure time (see, for example, Michelon, 1954).

Although this "antidote" may indeed be very good advice, it addresses only one aspect of the multi-faceted phenomenon of aging—that is, individual role loss. The prevailing gerontological paradigm preserves the traditional middle-class perspective vis-à-vis social problems—namely, that problems generally have both their causes and their solutions in *individual* human conduct. The key word here is individual. An example of this perspective can be found in Riesman (1950). Riesman explained the aging process as a function of personal fortitude and other psychological characteristics. In Riesman's typology, social structure is not considered; there are, simply, different aging types: the autonomous, the adjusted, and the anomic.[9]

This mode of typological analysis has since given way to more sophisticated analyses, although the focus remains on the level of the individual. Thus, although researchers may be less likely to construct theories in terms of personality "types" (such as, for example, the **rocking-chair** or **armored-defensive types** constructed by Reichard, Livson, and Peterson in 1962), they remain steadfast in their preference for developmental (individually oriented) role theories rather than role theories grounded in structural concepts, such as social class. A current interest of researchers, for example, is the synchronization of life events. In this research effort, the focus shifts from those who seem to be aging "normally" (or, at least, "on-time") to those who are occupying roles generally played by actors of a different age. Presumably, by understanding **"off-time"** or asynchronized aging patterns, we will learn

[9] Riesman's "adjusted" aging type includes those who "are the beneficiaries of a cultural preservative (derived from work, power, position, and so forth) that sustains them although only so long as the cultural conditions remain stable and protective" (1950, p. 164). It should be noted, however, that Riesman never fully elaborated the social-class implications of this oblique reference to extra-individual factors.

more about the large number of people who age normally.[10] Hogan, for example, has found that "deviant" ordering of life events is associated with marital disruption (1978); this suggests that marital harmony may be one of the positive outcomes of normative or "on-time" aging careers.

The conceptual rationale for much of the life-events literature is summarized nicely by Neugarten and Hagestad (1976), who argue that "age serves not only to rank persons hierarchically, but it serves also as the basis of prescribing, proscribing, or permitting various social roles" (p. 39). Current research in social gerontology focuses primarily on life-events studies. However, Neugarten, a major figure in this area, admits that the questions raised by this research "have no easy answers" (Neugarten & Hagestad, 1976, p. 52). She argues that more research is needed to document that "age-related changes in roles are not synchronized" (p. 48). Again, the emphasis here is clearly on the individual as an occupant of social roles. The view of aging suggested by this emphasis, to reiterate, is that aging is essentially an individually located problem, a challenge that each of us must face. The key to aging well is to remain synchronized with a prescribed blueprint, to remain on a certain developmental path or *chreod,* to use Back's (1976) term. This is vintage normative theory, displaying its penchant for phrasing its solutions to sociological problems in terms of individual adjustment which, in the present application, is adjustment to the rhythm of age-related changes in social roles.

Theories of Social Stratification

The two "sociologies" identified by Dawe as the normative and interpretive perspectives can also be discerned within the field of social stratification, a much older component of sociology than social gerontology. Social stratification has to do with the rules a society uses to distribute its resources, and it has occupied the attention of sociologists perhaps more than any other issue. In fact, the work of the 19th century "founding fathers" of European sociology has relevance for contemporary sociology mainly because of the way it addresses the important (and value-laden) issues of social mobility, class position, and class interests. For example, Marx contributed his brilliant insights into the role of social classes and class conflict in determining both economic *and* social position. Similarly, Weber's analyses of the economic *and* non-economic bases of stratification and the many dimensions of bureaucratically structured societies extended our understanding of social inequality. Emile Durkheim, although not generally considered to be a theorist of stratification, also contributed to debates of 20th century thinkers interested in stratification by his insistence that society is a reality "sui generis" and that order in

---

[10] For an overview of the life-events literature, see Hultsch and Plemons (1979). Other major articles focusing on the issues of asynchronization and life-course adaptation include Back (1976); Baltes and Willis (1977); Elder (1975); Hogan (1978); Levinson (1977); Neugarten (1969), and Neugarten and Datan (1973).

---

societies comes from mutually shared values—through consensus or **collective conscience** (1947). The bond that holds society together, according to Durkheim, is not power, subjugation, or class interests; rather, he believed that a system of shared symbols (commonly held values, for example) is the basis on which societies are maintained. Durkheim's belief in a collective conscience has evolved, in recent times, into the argument of functionalist theorists that social inequality is a result of the greater contribution to the commonweal made by upper-class citizens. Class position, in this view, is ultimately the result of individual characteristics like education, motivation, intelligence, or talent. The role of structural factors, like racial discrimination, or cultural barriers, like sex-role socialization or language incompatibility, are considered less important.

The Consensual Argument and Conflict Theory

Although Weber's multidimensional approach has been reflected in much of the empirical research in stratification (notably the **status inconsistency tradition** of research), the conceptual debate from 1940 through the present has focused on Durkheim's *consensual* argument versus the **conflict theory** of Marx. The debate between proponents of these opposing views was intensifed in 1945 by the appearance of an eight-page article entitled "Some Principles of Stratification" (Davis & Moore, 1945).

Davis and Moore, who represent Durkheim's *consensual* argument, based their article on the assumption that every society has to fill certain key positions that are required for the smooth functioning of the society. All members of a society, however, do not share the same talents and abilities, and a society must insure that its key positions are filled by its most capable members. Therefore, reasoned Davis and Moore, since positions vary in functional importance and individuals vary in ability, societies insure the appropriate matching of individual with position through the use of different rewards. That is, the most important positions attract the most competent individuals by offering the largest rewards (like, for example, large incomes).

The functionalist approach of Davis and Moore, when intially considered, impresses one as logically well-developed and certainly applicable to many instances in our everyday experience. Medical schools, for example, are rigorous training grounds for later practice, admitting only the best students and subjecting them to an intense and seemingly never-ending period of testing. The reward for completing this training is a large income and comfortable lifestyle. According to most rules of distributive justice, this reward seems fair, in addition to being rational. Rewards *should* be proportional to costs!

However, as Tumin pointed out in 1953, regardless of how rational such a stratification system may be, a nagging question remains as to the world it is intended to describe. It certainly does not describe industrial societies characterized by monopolistic capitalism. For example, if one presumes that an indvidual's position in the stratification hierarchy is determined by his or her abilities and/or contributions to the society, one must also presume that the explanation of social mobility (or lack of it) resides with the individual. It is this image of the "achievement" society that rankled Tumin and other critics of the functionalist stratification theory exemplified by Davis and Moore.

The functionalist perspective argues, in effect, that the major determinant of social position is individual ability. The failure of the functionalist approach to consider the possibility of structural barriers to mobility—including, for example, race and sex discrimination, unequal access to training and education, cultural "impediments" such as language problems and the lack of achievement-oriented role models—became the major target of the theory's critics.[11]

Functionalist theory embodies the major elements of Dawe's normative sociology perhaps like no other perspective before or since. With its emphasis on social order, rationality, and consensus, the theory conveys an image of society as clockwork, moving steadily through the time, sorting individuals into appropriate slots along the way in an efficient and objective manner. The *conflict* approach, on the other hand, although not identical to the interpretive approach, is clearly antithetical to the normative thesis of functionalism.

Conflict theory shares, perhaps more than any other perspective, interpretive sociology's concern that individuals regain control over social institutions. The problem of control occupies a central place in Marx's writings, particularly his writings on alienation, as well as in the works of 20th-century writers influenced by Marx, such as members of the Frankfurt school (for example, Horkheimer, Fromm, Adorno, and Marcuse) and "critical" theorists like Habermas. In the Marxist view, stratification systems are tools used by those in power to maintain their privileged positions; for instance, people in power may regulate access to educational and job-training opportunities in order to limit social mobility, which means, in effect, that public education preserves existing inequalities (Bowles, 1972). Ability, from this perspective, is a biological potential that occurs randomly among classes. The fact that social status is, for the most part, constant between different generations of the same families, attests to the structural impediments to developing natural abilities and talents.

Questions concerning the origins and persistence of stratification hierarchies continue to be raised, suggesting perhaps that neither the functionalist (consensual) nor the conflict argument alone provides a complete understanding of class-related phenomena. Some writers have contributed to a potential resolution of this problem by noting that Davis and Moore and the

[11] Major protagonists in the stratification debate include Buckley (1963), Davis (1959), Moore (1963), and Tumin (1963).

other functionalist writers probably never intended to imply that individuals are *naturally* sifted into slots that offer a level of reward compatible with individual ability (Stinchcombe, 1963). Although it is certainly true that some highly rewarded positions attract recruits by virtue of the size of the salary and the attractiveness of the fringe benefits, other positions offer low salaries and few fringe benefits but are filled nonetheless. This discrepancy can only be explained by incorporating into the functionalist theory factors viewed as structural impediments by the conflict theorists, such as the lack of viable job alternatives, or individual motives like job satisfaction. As it stands, function-alist theory can't explain the employment of some people in those positions "whose 'rewards'—if they may be called such—fall below the level of any-one's desires" (Bershady, 1970, p. 452).

Other writers have attempted to work out a synthesis between these two views by arguing that they are different sides of the same coin (van den Berghe, 1963); in other words, they are both valid. Lenski, for example, suggests that functionalist theory applies in those societies without an eco-nomic surplus where "the goods and services available will be distributed wholly, or largely, on the basis of need" (1966, p. 46). Conflict theory, according to Lenski, applies in those societies that are technologically ad-vanced and that produce an economic surplus. The surplus of any society is distributed to members not according to need but according to power.

The Status-Attainment and the Dual-Labor-Market Theories

To complete this brief overview of stratification theories, I should note that the syntheses of Lenski and other writers stilled the waters for only a brief period of time. The topics of stratification and social mobility, because they are so close to our vital everyday concerns and hopes, promise to be fertile grounds of intense debate for years to come. An illustration of the renewal of debate is the recent appearance of the opposing "**status-attainment**" and "**dual-labor-market**" theories.[12]

A major implication (and problem) of the status-attainment analyses of social mobility (see, for example, Featherman, 1972) is that mobility is large-ly a function of **"human capital"** or individual characteristics such as level of education. The dual-labor-market theorists, although they don't disagree that a portion of the observed variance in social mobility can be explained with human-capital variables, stress that an explanation of mobility must also take into account the existence of economic sectors and segmented labor markets; for example, recent analyses of social mobility have documented that Blacks

[12]Two similar theories dominate the interests of economists: the "human capital" and "dual economy" perspectives. The interested reader is directed to the works of Becker (1964; 1971) for the human capital perspective and to those of Averitt (1968) and Cain (1976) for the dual-economy point of view.

and women are disproportionately located in "peripheral" industries that are characterized by "small firm size, labor intensity, low profits, low productivity, intensive product market competition, lack of unionization, and low wages" (Bluestone, Murphy, & Stevenson, 1973, p. 28).

Dual-labor-market theorists argue that the dichotomization of industry into "core" and "periphery" sectors acts as a structural barrier to those workers whose sex or race tends to exclude them from higher paying jobs in "core" industries. In other words, even if the human-capital variables of education, work experience, and family background were equal, similar jobs would still be rewarded differently depending on their location in core or peripheral sectors. I will return to this issue in Chapter Four, where the situation of the older worker is considered.

In the case of the status-attainment and the dual-labor-market theories, as with the debate between the functionalist and conflict theorists, we see two sides of the same issue, neither of which tells the entire story. If one were a detached observer, complete with a value-free intelligence, it might be possible simply to meld the two views together and achieve both harmony *and* better theory. The possibility of creating such a broadminded perspective is too remote, however, to warrant more than passing reference; people's ideas are influenced too much by their social positions, and thus their observations are never truly objective or equally sensitive. In fact, the issue of whether science would even be well-served by a "detached intelligentsia" (to borrow a phrase from Mannheim) is open to question. My view is that it would not, because the confrontation of theories that reflect the different life experiences of their adherents is more likely than detached observation to produce the dynamic tension that can lead to deeper understanding.

In the chapters that follow, I will present a new perspective on the aging process that draws largely from both **exchange** and **symbolic interactionist theories.** For convenience, I will refer to this perspective as, simply, *exchange theory.* Although, in my view, exchange theory has greater utility than the dominant paradigm in gerontology, functionalist role theory, the reader may choose to see exchange theory as simply one more aspect of the topic of social gerontology. In any case, one must recognize that the development of an alternative point of view requires the prior existence of a different point of view or paradigm. For example, the emergence of the dual-labor-market theory is a phenomenon that cannot be understood without reference to the human capital theory, which preceded it. Similarly, an exchange view of aging must be placed in context of the dominance of role theory.

We have reviewed to this point several theoretical traditions within two broad sub-areas of sociology—namely, social gerontology and social stratification. We have discussed the extent to which the theoretical debate in each of these fields reflects the traditional clash between normative and interpretive points of view. Before we proceed to the major focus of the text, which is an application of exchange theory to the study of stratification among the aged, one preliminary task remains: we have yet to evaluate the state of research that deals with phenomena at the intersection of gerontology and stratification. Prior to presenting an exchange-theory view of these matters, the text will deal with research on aging that specifically addresses the subject of stratification and old people.

Aging and Social Class: Empirical Evidence

As I mentioned earlier in the chapter, the relationship between social class and aging truly merits our critical appraisal. With a few notable exceptions, however, the empirical studies relating to the issue of class and age effects suffer from severe methodological and conceptual shortcomings. The most notable of these exceptions is the landmark essay by Cain on "Life Course and Social Structure" (1964). In this piece, the author anticipated much of the sociological work on aging that would occur during the next sixteen years—including, for example, research on the topics of age stratification, legal-age status, age-group consciousness, and late-life socialization. Another major exception has been the work of Rosenberg on poverty, isolation, and the older worker (1968; 1970). Rosenberg has long argued that economic constraints on behavior do not cease to exist in old age; indeed, he sees old age as a time of life "in which class-related factors loom large . . . " (1968, p. 538). I share Rosenberg's view that it is certainly time that we "divest ourselves . . . of the idea of old age in the working class as a social limbo, of retirement as a beginning of an ineluctable separation of the aging man from society in the sense of the influence of his socioeconomic environment" (1968, p. 538).

Of the 18,000 articles on old age published between 1936 and 1956, only a handful were even tangentially concerned with old age *and* social class (Simpson, 1961), and the handful that was published added little to our understanding of stratification among the aged. This lack of research interest in the relationship between social class and old age continues to the present. Today, the research whose ostensible focus is social class and aging rarely gets beyond a mere description of attitudinal or value differences of old people from different social classes, and the measures of socioeconomic status used in these studies are questionable (cf. Nuttall & Fozard, 1970; Griffiths, Farley, Dean, & Boon, 1971; Trela, 1977–1978).

Studies of the working-class aged are also missing from the literature on social gerontology. With the exception of de Beauvoir's analysis in *The Coming of Age,* which suffers from its own problems of documentation and tendency toward overstatement, treatments of the working-class aged are generally written from a "consensus" perspective that emphasizes the similarities among classes over the obvious differences. Rose, for example, applies to a study of the aged what class theorists might term the **embourgeoisiement**

thesis (the view that the working classes in modern societies tend to adopt a middle-class style of life and world view):

> a large proportion of the older people today have the problems of the lower class. As American society is beginning to reduce these problems and to hold people in higher esteem, and as generational changes reduce some of the lower-class dominance among the elderly (for example, the proportion of the foreign-born is rapidly diminishing among the elderly) they will become relatively more like the middle class [1966, p. 356].

Rose is careful not to place older people within the working class; they only "have the problems" of the working or lower class. True to the middle-class American image of upward mobility, Rose then goes on to "solve" these problems through the magic of demographic transition, in which the poorer elements of society (the foreign-born) would disappear, leaving only the middle-class residue. Rose's treatment of class and the aged is not atypical; it reflects, rather, the same class background that is reflected in the work of the dominant figures in social gerontology. Indeed, much of the literature on aging is written by middle-class academicians whose middle-class grandparents apparently inspire much of the conceptualization and selection of research issues.

Viewing the aging process from the middle-class perspective of the academic researcher produces several interesting observations. For example, generations, as historical forces, are seen as cohesive entities wherein the members share similar values and economic position. Rosenmayr and Eder, for example, summarize a recent paper by Inglehart on generational change in values by noting that "the generation born after World War II, having been raised during a period of unprecedented prosperity, tend to give relatively high priority to nonmaterial goals; their parents and grandparents, having experienced hunger and turmoil during their formative years, remain likely to emphasize economic and physical security" (1978). Generalizations like this serve to obscure the tremendous differences that exist *within* each generation. The "generation" born after World War II, for example, includes members of different social classes and ethnicity—individuals to whom the generalization does not apply. One can only guess as to the reaction of the middle-aged member of the upper class on reading of his or her youthful hunger and turmoil-ridden existence, or, conversely, the reactions of the youthful sons and daughters of the factoryhand who learn that their adolescence was spent in a period of unprecedented prosperity that led them to develop their nonmaterial goals.

The point here is, of course, that each generation is composed of members from a variety of social-class, racial/ethnic and religious backgrounds. The tendency of middle-class academicians to ignore this internal differentation and proceed headlong into grand descriptions of entire generations ("the protest generation" or "the silent generation") makes for interesting journalism, perhaps, but violates basic principles of sociological analysis. The human community produces endless variation; it is this variation that should be the object of our inquiries.

Examples abound of the tendency to describe aging only in terms of the middle-class members of a particular age group, but space does not allow me to list all of them. I must note, however, the example of Streib's chapter on "Social Stratification and Aging" (1976). This work is excellent in most respects, but it does remark that "one of the paradoxes in later life is that persons can suffer severe declines in income, yet still retain essentially the same style of life" (p. 165). They are able to do this, he goes on to say, by careful budgeting and household management. Old people, for example, "take fewer and shorter vacations, drive their cars less, and buy a new model less frequently" (p. 165). Although gerontologists certainly recognize that many old people neither own a car nor take annual vacations, the disproportionate emphasis on those who do leaves the impression that the economic plight of our older citizens may be managed adequately by eliminating frills from the household budget.

In contrast to the image of the aged as middle-class, there is an equally biased view present in the gerontological literature that portrays the aged as destitute victims of an uncaring society. Popularized by newspaper reporters and textbook writers, this is the view of old age as a "social problem" (cf. Krauss, 1967; Tissue, 1970). Some stratification theorists, for example, argue that "increasingly, old age is a social problem, generated by long-range demographic and occupational trends and changes in social relationships" (Krauss, 1976, p. 183). This stereotype may help to account for the many studies that focus on the aged poor of the inner city—studies that highlight the poverty and danger that pervade the lives of these people (for example, Clark, 1971; Cohen & Sokolovsky, 1978; Lawton & Kleban, 1971; Lovald, 1961.)

I do not argue with the fact that many older people are forced to live in conditions of poverty and potential danger; I take issue with those studies that suggest that the aged as a group may be *characterized* as living under such conditions. We know this not to be the case. Not all working-class elderly live in the inner city. Pampel and Choldin, for example, noted recently (1978) that "the previous conception of the aged as highly segregated in inner-city ghettos is exaggerated." They go on to note that "although there are certainly older persons segregated in poor housing near the city center, they are not typical according to our data" (p. 1136).

In addition, not all aged residents of the inner city view their lives as necessarily requiring the attention of well-meaning geri-activists. For example, in a study of aged men living either in the downtown section of Sacramento or in the city's suburbs, Tissue (1971) found obvious differences in lifestyle between the two groups but, surprisingly, *no* differences in morale. Other reports document the ingenuity, vitality, and zest for life old people evidence regardless of where they are living (Rowles, 1978).

The danger of conceiving of old age as a social problem is that it promotes a *generalized* view of aging as a process leading to incapacitation,

---

poverty, and helplessness. Matthews (1977), in an insightful analysis of the ways in which old people attempt to cope with this "social problem" label, notes the case of one woman in her 60s who served on an advisory board to a local senior citizen's agency. Matthews describes her surprise at learning how bureaucrats tended to view the aged:

> Her assignment was to look into bills affecting older persons being considered in the state legislature. At the next meeting she commented that most of the bills were not just for the old, but also for the blind and disabled. She was amazed and incredulous that anyone would think it appropriate to lump the three groups together [p. 3].

Matthews goes on to argue that few among us would have shared this woman's amazement. Unfortunately, popular writings on the subject of aging tend to reinforce the notion "that to be old *is* to be handicapped" (p. 3).

A view of the aged that is related to the view of them as "social problems" is represented by the phrase "elderly mystique," which was coined by Rosenfelt (1965). The tenor of Rosenfelt's argument is that, because of modern technological change, we have stigmatized our old people as worthless and have abandoned them to live either alone or in age-segregated ghettos. By overgeneralizing from a selected sample, Rosenfelt grossly overstates her case and, in so doing, further confuses the issue. Rosenfelt argues, for example, that:

> Nothing is to be expected from the children. They have their own lives to lead. Furthermore, they are leading them, like as not, in distant locations, bridged only by the three-minute phone call on alternate Sundays, if contact is maintained at all [p. 39].

Given the mass of evidence indicating the frequent contact between old people and their adult children,[13] one can only conclude that Rosenfelt either is uninformed or neglected this evidence because it is inconsistent with her "elderly mystique" hypothesis.

Exchange Theory: An Alternative View of Aging as Exchange

In the chapters that follow, I will develop a view that has little in common with either the "social-problems" approach to old age or the biased middle-class view. I do not assume that old age is a homogeneous category. Neither do I assume that social classes lose their relevance or are leveled in old age. In fact, it is naive to attempt any characterization of the elderly without

---

[13] For information on degree of family contact see, for example, Adams, 1968; Britton, Mather, and Lansing, 1961; Rosenberg, 1970; Shanas, Townsend, Wedderburn, Friis, Milhog, and Stehouwer, 1968, Sussman, 1965; and Winch and Greer, 1968.

specifying their social/economic class. And, although it is admittedly difficult, when attempting to discuss the position of the aged within a specific historical context, not to rely upon a general description such as "devalued," statements such as "the aged are not needed by the community or their family as was true in earlier times" (Krauss, 1976) are unfounded.

Rather than presume that the life of the old person is invariably one either of despair due to poverty or of despondency due to role ambiguity, exchange theorists believe that the lives of the elderly are dependent largely on the relative power resources of the social actors involved. Thus, although exchange theorists recognize that old people in modern society tend to be disadvantaged because they generally possess fewer resources than young people, these theorists also recognize that there are exceptions; individuals often manipulate in outrageously innovative ways the few resources they do possess. Thus, although the long-term "exchange" view recognizes that possession of resources leads to power in social relationships, the short-term view appreciates the creative ability of humans to use resources in unique ways.

The exchange view of aging that is presented in the pages that follow derives essentially from the second of Dawe's two sociologies, the interpretive tradition. Stratification processes in old age will be examined in relation both to the constraints that status characteristics place on old people's behavior and to the voluntary actions of old people that modify existing "institutional imperatives" (to borrow a phrase from Berger & Luckmann). Some basic assumptions underlying the exchange approach to aging include the following:

1. The organization of a society reflects the interests of the dominant strata (social classes) within a stratification hierarchy.
2. Dominant strata attempt to maintain favorable institutional arrangements (that is, the greater access of members of the dominant strata to political, economic, and educational systems) through the exercise of power.
3. The legitimacy attached to institutional arrangements by older people is effected through a process of socialization; however, because socialization is always limited in scope and never totally effective, the legitimacy granted to existing arrangements may be withdrawn.

The presentation begins with a consideration of structure and proceeds to a consideration of the individual; specifically, it starts with problems in the social system and then goes on to the ways in which the individual old person negotiates (or fails to negotiate) a viable existence within the structure. Along the way, we will need to come to grips with a diversity of issues, ranging from the macroproblems of modernization and the declining status of the aged to the microlevel concerns of justice, alienation, identity, and age-group consciousness.

Our discussion will close with a consideration of several issues with implications both for social policy and basic research. Among these issues are: whether present or future cohorts of old people will develop a cohesive sociopolitical organization capable of effecting a more favorable quality of life for the aged; the continued separation of age groups in our society through segregated housing facilities; the adequacy of existing social-support systems for the aged; and, finally, the nature of social interaction in old age and the meaning attributed to these interactions by old people themselves.

Review Questions

1. *Compare the functionalist and conflict theories of stratification.*
2. *Is it a simplification to say that people are nothing but the roles and statuses they occupy? (In thinking about this question, consider the normative and interpretive points of view presented by Dawe.)*
3. *Define the difference between competitive and monopolistic capitalism.*
4. *What are some of the differences between the disengagement and activity theories of aging? Do you think the two theories have any points in common?*
5. *How are ideas and social class related?*
6. *What is the "elderly mystique," and how is this term misused?*

2

Age,
Class,
and
Social
Inequality

The personal troubles associated with growing old are experienced earlier and more frequently among those at the bottom of the class hierarchy than among those at the top. This simple observation is not made clear, however, in recent analyses of age stratification that relate age and class only inasmuch as they constitute two distinct means of analyzing social status. Foner and Kertzer (1978), for example, propose to analyze rites of passage and generational succession in terms of "age conflicts and tensions" just as Marx analyzed social change in terms of class conflict. Although the age-stratification literature has contributed much to our understanding of age-related phenomena, we must eventually move beyond the restrictions imposed by this approach and attempt to integrate the concepts of age stratum *and* social class within a single perspective. In reality, the social world resists such facile categorization as the arrangement of stratification hierarchies in neat, discrete, juxtaposed columns marked "age" and "class"; but it is my contention that the individual experience of growing old and the nature of age relations vary so significantly by social class that there is a need for unified analysis in which both age *and* class are considered.

It is also necessary to integrate the concepts of age stratum and social class when one examines issues that encompass more than the relations and problems of individuals. For example, the problems of inequality of social classes within a particular age stratum (class stratification) and inequality of different age strata (age stratification) involve the same issue; if one talks about inequality in one case, one will have to touch on inequality in the other. This is not to suggest that age stratification and class stratification share similar origins or persist for similar reasons. However, both age strata and social classes are defined by the possession or lack of valued resources and the degree of access to the means of acquiring these resources. As a result, membership in a particular age stratum or social class facilitates a certain style of life and world-view.

Interaction patterns are also affected by the stratum or class membership of the actors involved: interaction among people of equal status proceeds from a basis of greater common understanding and is, therefore, potentially less structured than interaction involving actors from different classes or strata. In other words, interaction among status equals is less likely to involve the exercise of **deference.** In studies of social class, the actors involved are usually about the same age; in studies of age stratification, the principal parties are of different ages. However, deference means the same in both cases: one actor (individual or group) defers to the greater power of another. The key element is neither age nor social class but the *power* that one's age and social status confer.

One similarity between social class and age stratum, then, lies in the fact that both affect an individual's access to wealth, power, and status. In other words, age and social class have independent but compounding effects on power and privilege. Another similarity lies in the fact that individuals do not compete in these dual stratification systems for different rewards; rather, the same prize is at stake in each—power. And, as it stands today, within a particular social class, the middle-aged members typically have greater resources and, therefore, greater power than either the young or the old. Likewise, among members of a particular age **stratum,** the middle-class members exercise greater power then the working-class members.

Relations between *some* youth and *some* parents (or between some old people and some middle-aged people) seem to approximate the relations between social classes, which have been defined by Lenski (1966) as aggregates "of persons in a society who stand in a similar position with respect to some form of power, privilege, or prestige" (p. 75). The age of the participants is not the source of the conflict frequently observed between generations; conflict occurs over the unequal distribution of resources and the desire of one group to effect a redistribution of resources in its favor.

One of the reasons, perhaps, why both social gerontologists and social-stratification specialists have been so reluctant to address the issues involved in an analysis of old age and social stratification is the ambiguity of the social-class membership of the aged. Time and again, analysts of mobility patterns are forced to exclude those over the age of 65 due to lack of occupational data for this group. Similarly, even those interested in generational relationships exclude the aged from their analyses, for, as one group of researchers reported, old people have "left the active phase of life and need not be considered anymore" (Carlsson & Karlsson, 1970, p. 714). This problem has its roots in the Marxist analysis of social class, in which classes are defined by their members' relationship to means of production. In capitalist political economies, the two major social classes are, of course, the bourgeoisie and the proletariat—those who own or control the means of production and those who sell their labor for wages.

Recent neo-Marxist definitions of social class, although they modify somewhat Marx's original definition, extend the concept in order to take into account the changes in capitalist economies since the time of Marx's writings. Neo-Marxists such as Wright and Perrone (1977) operationally define four social classes—capitalists, managers, workers, and petite bourgeoisie—based on four related criteria: (1) ownership of the means of production; (2) purchase of the labor power of others; (3) control of the labor power of others (for example, foremen, office supervisors); and (4) sale of one's own labor power. Even though Marx's definition of social class has been expanded, it remains unclear where the aged fit. The mandatory retirement policies of many large corporations make it unlikely that old people would qualify as managers or even workers (except as part-time older workers). It is certain, however, that those in the capitalist class (the rich), upon passing the age of 65, do not become proletarianized but become, rather, old capitalists. Similarly, the old couple who run the "Ma and Pa" grocery store remain clearly among the petite **bourgeoisie.** The problem cases, therefore, are most women and retired males who make up the large bulk of the population we are interested in! Where do they fit in?

One solution is to assign to old people the class designations they would have if they were still working at the jobs they held most of their lives. There are sound reasons for doing this. Research on status attainment in old age suggests that status is still largely determined by the same variable that predicted income in mid-life—namely, education. In other words, if class is defined in terms of income, there is a good deal of continuity in relative ranking from mid-life to old age since education remains fairly constant across the life cycle. In fact, Henretta and Campbell (1976) suggest that old age should be characterized as a time of status "maintenance" rather than status "attainment."

The major problem with assigning old people to a particular class on the basis of the occupations they held in midlife is that such assignment disregards the reality of old age as experienced by most old people. The aged are removed from the "dull compulsion of economic relations" that Marx saw as central to the persistence of the class hierarchy. The aged, for the most part,

---

no longer exchange their labor for a wage; their survival no longer depends on their participation in the workplace. By this simple fact, it would be difficult to describe old people as belonging to the "working" class (they do not "work") or even to the middle class, since the aged's "interests" are no longer shaped solely by economic relations. Although the *retired* executive, for example, generally does not refuse an increase in his Social Security allotment, this same increase may produce considerable annoyance, if not outright hostility, in the middle-aged executive whose FICA tax has been raised to cover the additional benefits.

Previous efforts to apply a class analysis to the aged have been somewhat disappointing because of a failure to grasp the continuity underlying the inequality produced by age and class location. From an analysis of their cross-national study of old people, for example, Shanas and her colleagues (1968) are able to conclude only that the aged comprise "a kind of potential or embryonic 'class.'" Neugarten and Hagestad point out that this is really just "one way of saying that it is not clear where the old are to be ranked in relation to other age categories" (1976, p. 37). Rather than attempt to clarify the age-class relationship, however, Neugarten and Hagestad admit that they, like most researchers, "know very little about the way in which age criteria actually operate alongside other criteria in determining social rank." This confusion results from a failure to recognize that, although class and age stratification can be *conceptualized* as distinct phenomena, it becomes ludicrous to attempt to separate "age interests" from "class interests" for any one person. This is not to deny the existence of social classes or age groups, but we must not be led to consider the terms *age group* and *social class* to mean mutually exclusive groups of people or to have a reality beyond their descriptive role.

Relevant to this discussion of age, social class, and power is Homan's suggestion that we "bring men back in" our theories and conceptualizations. If we think of individuals like you and me, the clouds obscuring these issues drift away; what we see is real people in the midst of life's everyday events, attempting to obtain the most rewarding, least costly, possible outcomes. From this perspective, the unit of analysis is social interaction; the principal variable, and reward, is power. When an old person interacts with others, regardless of whether it is with other old people or younger persons, power is being exercised through the exchange of resources. In some situations, the old person is disappointed by the outcome. Other interactions are welcomed because they are perceived as rewarding. In any case, power is based on the ownership of exchange resources; and the inequalities that exist among age or social-class groups are maintained by possession of power.

Before elaborating in more detail the perspective on age relations offered by exchange theory, I will discuss briefly other ways in which social scientists have approached the issue of age relations. A review of the relevant literature suggests at least three different approaches to this issue: (1) the sociobiological; (2) the psychoanalytic; and (3) the structural-functional.

The number of studies conducted on age/strata relationships from a sociobiological perspective is rather small; this is because the sociobiological approach to age relations is fairly new, and there is resistance to it among anthropologists, sociologists, and social psychologists who do not adhere to the concept of genes or instincts as determinants of behavior.[1] The focus of much of the sociobiologists' concern has been on the degree of cooperation and conflict among parents and their offspring. Trivers, for example, sees the behavior of nursing mothers as determined by the same genes that later lead the grown-up child to care for the aging parent (1971). At the same time, however, Trivers (1974) also posits the existence of genes that are responsible for parent/child conflict. Dawkins (1976) similarly refers to generational relations as being influenced by a "selfish gene." The selfish gene is posited as the basis for the eternal conflict between parents and children: the parents want to insure the health of a maximum number of offspring in order to propagate as many of their genes as possible in future generations. At the same time, however, each child is concerned mostly with his or her own survival and, consequently, is in a situation of continuous competition with siblings (and, hence, in a traditional home situation, in a continuous struggle with the mother) for a disproportionate share of the mother's resources (milk, for example).

The conflict between generations worried some observers several years ago so much that they introduced a new term to describe it—the generation "gap." This "gap" has been given an "instinct" explanation by the zoologist Lorenz (1970); he writes, somewhat hysterically, that what the youth of the 1960s was actually doing was "indulging in the archaic instinctual pleasure of tribal war, waged against the parent generational. The hate that they bear us—the older generation—is in the nature of national hatred of the most stultifying of all emotions" (1970, p. 338).

To my knowledge, most of the sociobiologist's concern has been with the parent/child relationship and has not systematically focused on the child/grandparent or parent/grandparent relations. Several papers have appeared recently, however, that attempt a sociobiological explanation for the variable treatment accorded old people in different cultures. From a sociobiological view, the existence of old people is itself an anomaly. Of all the primates, only humans tend to live well past their reproductive years (Katz, 1978). Since the aged in most societies tend to be dependent for their support upon younger members of the group and since they possess little reproductive value, the question raised by the sociobiologists is why have old people

---

[1] For a thorough introduction to the general field of sociobiology, the works of E. O. Wilson (1975; 1978) are highly recommended.

"succeeded" in human populations? Some researchers argue that the increasing longevity over the course of human history "must be connected to the social contribution each aged parent makes toward stabilizing the cultural traditions of their offpsring and insuring continuity of sociocultural adaptations" (Katz, 1978, p. 5). This is similar to the notion of reciprocal altruism argued by Trivers (1971). According to these researchers, older people survive because they provide an important service to the group, such as help in the rearing of grandchildren or the offpsring of relatives, or help in food gathering or production of materials (Feinman, 1979). This position receives some support from cross-cultural data on the status of old people (which will

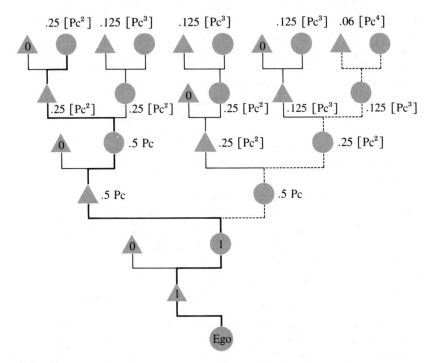

FIGURE 2-1. Possible pathways of descent for a female's paternally derived X chromosome and the attendant probabilities that a gene on Ego's X chromosome will be identical by descent with that of the ancestor. $p = \frac{1}{2}^x$ [Pc^x], where x is the number of female ancestors on the path and Pc is the probability of loss by crossover. Solid line, most likely lines of descent; dotted line, least likely line of descent. As Li and Sacks (1954, p. 354) have pointed out in reference to sex-linked genes, "the relationship between paternal grandmother and granddaughter is the same as that between mother and daughter." Adapted from "On Natural Selection and the Inheritance of Wealth," by J. Hartung, Current Anthropology, 1976, 17, 607–622. Copyright 1977 by the University of Chicago. Reprinted by permission.

be reviewed in Chapter Four). These data suggest that whenever old people are incapable of providing some useful service or when it becomes too expensive for the group to "purchase" these services (due to resource shortage, for example), the aged not only lose status but are likely to be ostracized from the group (Glascock & Feinman, 1978).

Another hypothesis to explain the "success" of old people—a hypothesis as yet untested—suggests that **patrilocal** or **patrilineal** societies are more likely to support the existence of old people than other types of societies (Katz, 1978). Since the X chromosome is suspected of contributing more to longevity than the Y chromosome, it is argued that any social mechanism that increases the chances for survival of any X chromosome will contribute to postreproductive longevity. Patrilocality is one such mechanism since it permits the *grandmother* to care for her son's daughters. In patrilocal societies, it is customary for a married couple to reside in the vicinity of the home of the husband's parents; such an arrangement allows an older (postmenopausal) female to "increase her genetic representation among her grandchildren's generation by taking preferential care of her son's daughter" (Katz, 1978, p. 5.) Since the chances are twice as great that a grandmother will contribute one of her X chromosomes to her son's daughters than to her daughter's daughter, any social arrangement that facilitates interaction between a female child and her paternal grandmother increases the survival chances of the group. From this contribution to the group's longevity, the functional importance of grandparents (at least grandmothers) is derived. To illustrate the basic genetic principles involved in this theory, Figure 2-1 gives the possible pathways of descent for a female's paternally derived X chromosome.

In any case, the value of the sociobiological approach to the study of age relations and social interaction appears inherently limited to those interactions in which the participants share a common gene pool. Although I would be interested in seeing evidence to the contrary, it seems to me that the potential of the sociobiological approach to the study of stratification and aging appears fairly limited.

The Psychoanalytic View

The view that I refer to as *psychoanalytic* shares the sociobiological approach's tendency to frame explanations of generational relations within an individualistic context.[2] Historical or social-structural forces appear in these

---

[2]Indeed, in some writers, the two views are indistinguishable. Lorenz (1970), for example, who believes that generational conflict has its basis in an instinct for tribal warfare, also notes that this tribal war between generations is caused by "a mass neurosis." He goes on to note that this psychiatric diagnosis is "less pessimistic than it seems, because neurosis, in principle, has a chance of being cured by making its subconscious roots accessible to conscious understanding" (1970, p. 338).

accounts—if they appear at all—as secondary to the universal force of competition between fathers and sons that was identified by Freud as **oedipal rebellion:** Youth rebel against middle-aged authority because of the deep-rooted and unresolved hostility toward their fathers and the guilt resulting from a suppressed desire to murder them. This theme is developed most thoroughly in Feuer's controversial study, entitled *The Conflict of Generations* (1969). It is Feuer's view, as it was noted in an excellent review of the **generations** literature by Spitzer (1973), that the "recognition of the oedipal springs and the parricidal guilt of the generational rebellion helps us to understand the self-sacrificing idealism, the populism, and the murderous and suicidal irrationalism of militant youth movements" (p. 1365).

Other versions of the psychoanalytical approach have been argued by Lowenberg (1971), who attempted to explain the emergence of the Nazi youth cohort in Germany during the 1930s, and by Esler (1971), who applied the psychoanalytical approach in an explanation of generational relations in France during the 1830s. Although both authors recognize the importance of the social-historical contexts of their studies, they both stress the need for a psychoanalytical framework to understand the areas under examination. Lowenberg in particular stresses the need for a psychoanalytical framework to understand the pathology of Nazism. He seeks his explanation for the rise in Nazism in the trauma of World War I that was visited upon the generation born between 1900–1910 and that later manifested itself as "aggression, defenses of projection and displacement, and inner rage," and, ultimately, a "preference for extremist paramilitary political organizations" (1971, p. 1501).

More recently, psychohistorians have questioned the validity of the **Oedipus complex** as an explanation for youthful protest, preferring instead the more esoteric **Rustum complex.** As described by Sheleff (1976), the Rustum Complex is derived from a Persian myth in which Rustum, a famous warrior, "kills his son, Sohrab, in face-to-face single combat, and to his grief discovers their kinship only as the son's life is ebbing away, victim of his father's weapon" (p. 24). The Rustum myth presumably goes beyond the Oedipus story since it shows that "parents, too, have a built-in antagonism toward their progeny" (Sheleff, p. 29).

From a sociological perspective, the value of the psychoanalytic approach to research in age relations is highly questionable. It is dfficult to presume the existence of universal, intra-individual wellsprings of unresolved antagonisms in all young people; it is almost impossible to believe the same thing on the part of old people. However, this is not to say that sociologists do not on occasion resort to psychoanalytic theories. In order to fit their structural explanations into those treacherous places where sociological concepts appear ill-suited, sociologists occasionally resort to psychological theories. In order to explain the decline in status that accompanies old age, for example, Streib (1976) offers the younger generations' fear of death as a relevant factor.

Because young people fear their own demise, the group of persons closest to death—the aged—are also feared and, therefore, despised. However, because of the absence of data supporting this hypothesis and those similar to it, the psychoanalytic approach appears at this time to be little more than speculative, albeit provocative.

The Structural-Functional Approach

The structural-functional approach to generational analyses is most closely associated with the development by Riley, Johnson, and Foner (and other collaborators including Waring, Starr, Hess, Nelsen, and Parelius) of a "sociology of age stratification" (1972). Although Riley's discussion of her model of age stratification contains numerous references to class stratification (in an attempt to draw out the points of convergence and contrast), the Riley approach is clearly functional in orientation. By this, I mean essentially that Riley and her collaborators view society as an ordered, rational structure—constituted of roles, norms, and an Adam-Smith-like "invisible hand"[3] —that allocates individuals to appropriate age-graded slots. The functionalist view, in the classic sociological tradition of Durkheim, is strongly deterministic in its perception of behavior as primarily role-bound.

The age-stratification theorists argue that age, like class, forms the basis of a system of stratification. However, in spite of references to Marx and analogies to class stratification, it is Parsons and Merton, not Marx, who have inspired the theory of age stratification. In this case, the interest lies not in conflict and power but in roles and norms. Age defines strata not because society's economic surplus is distributed differently to dominant and subordinant age strata, but because, as Foner (1975) notes, "age orders both people and roles." The life course is viewed by Riley as a series of related roles, joined together by their linkage with chronological age, and behavior is explained in terms of incumbency in age-related roles. The individual is not described in terms of creative ability or autonomy but rather in terms of the group of people who were born around the same time as the individual and who share similar experiences. As Foner explains, "all roles have built-in age

---

[3] In 1776, a Scottish philosopher, Adam Smith, authored a book *(Wealth of Nations)* that presented an economic model known ever since as classical or "laissez-faire" economics, from the French phrase "allow to do as one pleases." Smith believed that free competition in the marketplace would result in lower prices and higher standards of living for all. Government intervention, in the form of tariffs, restrictions, subsidies, or regulations, is, in Smith's view, counterproductive. If people were left to their own devices, the net result would be beneficial to all—just as if some god-like, invisible hand coordinated the actions of each person.

---

definitions of role assignment and expectations and rewards for role performance" (1975, p. 147).

It is difficult to find fault with many of the points of the age-
stratification model. It is certainly true, for example, that age affects attitude
and behavior and that individuals from different age strata "have unequal
opportunities to gain desired positions." However, Riley's preoccupation with
roles and rules leads to a deemphasis of the individual's effect on the social
system that is not so easy to accept. In her view, it is the system and its
remarkable ability to allocate roles and socialize individuals that are the objects requiring study. Those who scream back at the world that they refuse to
"act their age" are transmogrified in this model to age deviants, the "passers"
in the age-stratification hierarchy (Nelsen & Nelsen, 1972).

Researchers' disappointment in Riley's treatment of age stratification
(1971, 1973, 1974) stems from the fact that she fails to nurture this promising
child. The members of the Riley-Foner group certainly recognize the potential
for conflict inherent in age relations, but they seem not to know quite what to
make of it. Foner (1975) admits, for example, that "what is not firmly established are the conditions that give priority to age ties as compared to class,
sex, race, or ethnic bonds" (p. 159). Similarly, Riley (1976) hints that the
relations among generations may not always proceed according to design
—for instance, when "divergence in values . . . leads to change through
outright conflict" (p. 211). Rather than pursue this notion by suggesting
examples of potential value conflict, Riley (1976) returns to the more familiar
ground of reified role theory as she focuses on

> aging and the succession of cohorts that follow their own rhythm, that entail
> special processes and structures for allocation and socialization of personnel,
> and that in themselves constitute strains and pressures toward "innovation"
> [p. 215].

Riley's Influence on the Sociology of Age

The influence of the age-stratification model within sociology and
social gerontology is characterized by the model's great breadth and shallow
depth. That is, the legacy of Riley's approach has been to sensitize researchers
in these fields to the importance of "structural" factors such as cohort size and
the intricate interconnection of successive cohorts, which is important to both
society and the individual. Yet, at the same time, the model has not generated
any testable hypotheses to send researchers scurrying to design appropriate
tests and measures. The influence of the age-stratification model has also been
more general than specific; for example, because of Riley's pioneering

efforts, we have recognized that a life-span sociology must eventually replace an exclusive interest in gerontology.[4]

The age-stratification model has had a tremendous impact on the empirical analysis of **age, period,** and **cohort effects.** In the course of developing her theory of stratification, Riley incorporated the earlier work of psychologists and demographers on age and cohort effects. Intrigued by the work of Ryder (1965; 1972) on the role of age groups (birth cohorts) as forces of historical or cultural change, Riley sought to adapt the concept of *cohort* to her interest in the socialization of generations to values and norms. Riley's contribution to the cohort issue—termed the *problem of generations* decades earlier by Mannheim—was the perception that ontogenetic change in humans (biological development) only partially accounts for observed changes related to aging. Indeed, Riley recognized that some of the age-related changes that had been considered to be the result of ontogeny were actually the result of differences among birth *cohorts*—differences in demographic composition and historical experience.

Riley's analysis of this issue, with only minor exceptions,[5] proved to be a great contribution to the empirical research efforts on the effects of human aging. She made gerontologists aware that the relative impact of historical events on the individual depends to some degree on the social location and life-stage position of the individual. In other words, Riley understood that people of different ages experience the same historical event in a qualitatively dissimilar fashion. Unlike the empirical analyses that were published prior to the third volume in the *Aging and Society* series (1972), the later analyses of generations evidenced the understanding that change, over time, cannot simply be traced to one of the three APC (age-period-cohort) effects but is a function of all three components.[6]

Since the Riley age-stratification model for the study of generations and aging has only been available for a short time, it is still too soon to assess the extent of its influence. However, because of the continued high representation in sociological and gerontological journals of authors conveying the

---

[4] Although there is as yet no body of research that may be dubbed the "age stratification literature," the original core of professors and students from Rutgers, the State University of New Jersey, who collaborated on the *Aging and Society* trilogy, continue to write spin-off articles that show the age-stratification influence. For a sampling of articles from the Rutgers group, the reader is directed to Foner (1974; 1978); Foner and Kertzer (1978); Parelius (1975); and Waring (1975).

[5] As discussed by Palmore (1978), Riley confused matters somewhat with her penchant for referencing an additional (fourth) element to the now familiar aging-period-cohort set. Riley refers to this additional factor as "age strata" differences.

[6] The literature on the empirical analysis of generations is too large to summarize here in a short note. The interested reader, however, may wish to compare the pre-1972 work that emphasized one of the three APC effects (see, for example, Crittenden, 1962; 1963; and Cutler, 1969) with the post-1972 studies that tend to stress an integration of the three age-related effects (Agnello, 1973; Cutler & Kaufman, 1975; Douglass, Cleveland, & Maddox, 1974; Jennings & Niemi, 1975; and Knoke & Hout, 1974).

age-stratification point of view, at least a preliminary evaluation of the model appears warranted. In my view, the Riley model's impact on social-gerontological research in the 1970s can be compared to the effect of Cumming and Henry's landmark monograph, *Growing Old*, a decade or so earlier. In each case, although the intent of the authors was to present a theoretical statement, the importance of the study was observed in its application to research design, methodological strategy, and selection of variables.

Although there are only a few, if any, disengagement theorists today, the analysis of activity patterns and predictors of life satisfaction go on and on. There are also few age-stratification or functionalist theorists to be identified outside of the original Rutgers group; yet this group continues to influence the APC literature, which displays a tradition of research that is noted for its empirical, or quantitative, contributions. Unlike the frequent misinterpretations (or fallacies, as Riley refers to them) of age-related data common in the literature of the 1960s, most of the recent studies have at least attempted to control for each of the three effects.

Not all of the problems inherent in cohort analyses have been resolved, however. Some studies continue to misinterpret cross-sectional data on age effect, because they don't investigate the possibility of cohort-related differences. Others analyze longitudinal data without attempting to distinguish age effects from period effects. More frequent, however, is the tendency to view age, period, and cohort effects as mutually exclusive rather than contemporaneous effects. Particularly in those analyses that employ what Mason, Mason, Winsborough, and Poole (1973) term the *ransacking method,* the authors typically couch the analysis in terms of "which *one* of the three effects is operative?" (See, for example, Bengtson & Cutler, 1976; Cutler & Bengtson, 1974; and Dalton, 1977.) This tendency should diminish, however, as future analyses adopt one of the more recent research techniques, all of which allow an assessment of multiple causation. Promising beginnings in the refinement of research technique were pioneered by Mason and her colleagues (1973) and Palmore (1978) in the analysis of age effects (cf. Glenn, 1976).

In addition to influencing the study of age within the field of sociology, Riley also influenced research on social dynamics in the area of social history. Actually, historians and political scientists have long expressed interest—based on Mannheim's essay on the problem of generations (1952) —in the concept of historical or political generations. The period since 1972 has seen sociologists join the political historians in their interest in generations as sociohistorical forces.[7] Riley's contribution to the study of social dynamics came about through her awareness of the methodological difficulties involved

[7]For examples of some of the early work in this area, see Berger (1960); Browder (1969); Cain (1967); Eisenstadt (1956; 1971); Eros (1955); Gusfield, (1957); Inglehart (1967; 1971); Lewytzkyj (1967); Lutz (1962); Newman (1939); Ortega y Gasset (1958); Rintala (1958; 1963); Simirenko (1966); Treves (1964); and Zeitlin (1970). A sample of the recent literature includes Balswick (1974); Ben-David (1973); Gieryn (1977); Hellman (1975); Horn (1973); Jones (1974); Lieberson (1973); Nagel (1975); Pye (1977); Wheeler (1974); and Wuthnow (1976),

in the empirical analysis of APC effects, particularly the problem of disentangling each of the three effects (the "identification" problem). For this reason, rather than using date-of-birth information as a tool for precise measurement in statistical analysis, Riley suggested the use of age data in a descriptive or exploratory way in research on social dynamics. This suggestion is consistent with Riley's admiration of Ryder's (1965) analysis of the effect of cohort flow in the process of social change. Thus, some researchers may argue that Riley's greatest influence has been among social historians who have recently redoubled their persistent interest in historical generations.

As suggested earlier, however, there is a major *theoretical* problem with the Riley model—that is, its failure to adequately integrate the effects of class with those of age. It has become evident that, empirically, age variables alone do not totally explain the variance of social-psychological or sociological phenomena. Although some studies using this model do report interpretable patterns of age, period, and cohort effects, when these effects are included in analyses *along with* traditional measures of status—including income, race, occupation, and education—the proportion of explained variance attributable to the APC effects is miniscule (Knoke & Hout, 1974). In other words, in order for maturation or other age-related variables—like cohort membership or period effects—to contribute to our understanding of behavior, they *must* be integrated with measures of social class.

This proviso gains added significance when one realizes that age may well lose its significance as one travels the life cycle. The observation that a one-year difference in age is more significant among children than among adults is freighted with significance for sociologists interested in aging. The defining characteristics of a cohort most likely are imprinted during the initial confrontation with the existing social structure (compare Mannheim's "fresh contact" notion). Although the effect of this initial confrontation may well persist as long as there are living members of that cohort, the *differences* between that cohort and those adjacent to it tend to decrease over time. This is hardly surprising, given the amount of exposure, over time, of adjacent cohorts to the same historical events. Some theorists suggest, in fact, that the largest differences between any two adjacent five-year birth cohorts are probably those that exist between the 25–29 age group and the 30–34-year-olds (Carlsson & Karlsson, 1970).

The inference from these data is not that homogeneity *within* generations (or age cohorts) necessarily increases over time. It is clear that there is tremendous internal variation among individuals within older cohorts as well as within younger cohorts. The conclusion suggested by these studies is, rather, that an age-stratification model may best be used in analyses of the interaction among younger cohorts (parent-youth conflict, for example).[8] Studies of the interaction among older cohorts, on the other hand, require a

[8] For an excellent review of generational analyses of youth, see Bengtson, Furlong, and Laufer (1974).

consideration of the distribution of power and privilege within, as well as between, age strata (cohorts), and it is this necessary integration of class and age effects that the Riley age-stratification model fails to provide.

Power and Deference: Basis of a Rapprochement between Age and Class

Aging, as argued by de Beauvoir (1972), is a class struggle. When this thesis was first argued, the concept was difficult to understand; it remains difficult today. The reason we resist thinking of old people as a social class is largely terminological: age and class, as most writers have told us, are separate systems. The need to keep these concepts separate has, in my view, curtailed the utility of each. In order to achieve any integration of the two, we must first look for one factor that is of concern to both systems: one such factor is power.

Power, viewed from the perspective of the stratification theorist, involves the ability to get what one wants and "to influence others in ways that further one's own interests" (Parenti, 1978, p. 12). As we shall see in the next chapter, this use of the term *power* differs somewhat from the way exchange theorists use the term; according to exchange theorists, power is the state of relative independence that results from having a greater share of valued resources than one's exchange partner. However, the two uses are actually complementary rather than contradictory: one is intended to describe the relations among 'groups (the stratification definition), whereas the other applies to the relations among individuals (the exchange definition). Earlier, I referred to social classes in Lenski's terms as aggregates whose members stand in a similar position with respect to some form of power, privilege, prestige or institutionalized force (authority). Although definitions of social class vary from writer to writer,[9] the factor of access to power underlies all of them. This factor gives significance to the concepts of class and stratification. Rothman (1978), for example, although he made a point of distinguishing between the terms *inequality* and *stratification,* was unable to define either without referring to power: inequality is the uneven distribution of any resource, including power, whereas stratification means the relatively permanent "power arrangements" (as well as the values, beliefs, and ideas) that both underlie and result from structured inequalities.

I would suggest that, just as class and stratification resist being defined without a similar reference, definitions of age stratification are not complete

[9] See, for example, the definitions of class as supplied by Abrahamson, Mizruchi, and Hornung (1976); Bottomore (1968); Eisenstadt (1971); Jackson and Curtis (1968); Krauss (1967); and McCord and McCord (1977).

without reference to power. The meaning of de Beauvoir's bold assertion that "aging is a class struggle" becomes clear when one begins to think of both aging and class in terms of power. Although neo-Marxist writers may disagree with any use of the word *class* that fails to specify a group's relationship to the means of economic production in a society, I concur with Dahrendorf's more pragmatic argument that "there is no reason why we should not call quasi-groups and interest groups classes or anything else" (1959, p. 201). Clearly the aged are not a social class if we take the "realist" position regarding their existence. Such a view holds social classes to be "groups possessed both of real and vital common economic interests and of a group-consciousness of their general position in the social scale" (Marshall, quoted in Wrong, 1964). Aging may be viewed as a class struggle, however, if one holds the opposing "nominalist" view of social classes. According to this position, class refers to a group of individuals who share certain attributes (the individuals do not need to be aware of their common bonds, however). Paraphrasing Dahrendorf's much-quoted definition of social classes, we can state that age strata are essentially "social conflict groups, the determinant of which can be found in the participation in or exclusion from the exercise of authority" (1959, p. 138). I would modify this definition by adding "and the exercise of *power* and control of *power resources.*"

Although it departs from the neo-Marxists' strict definition of class, the view of social class and aging proposed here does share conflict theory's concern with the ways in which unequal access to power resources determines social status and life chances. Unlike the functionalists, who insist that the distribution of rewards in a society is a function of individual abilities, the conflict theorists recognize that rewards are distributed as a function of power. This theme is elaborated in Lenski's monograph, *Power and Privilege.*[10] Lenski argued that both cooperation and conflict are present in all societies to varying degrees. However, in societies that have a large economic surplus (modern industrial societies), it is conflict, or power, that largely determines the distribution of the surplus.

An economic surplus may be defined as what a group produces "in excess of what is needed to keep the producers healthy and productive" (Lenski & Lenski, 1978, p. 153). Until the discovery of the basic techniques of animal domestication and farming around 10,000 B.C. (the Neolithic Revolution), economic production was limited to hunting and gathering. With the development of horticulture, the first economic surplus was created. This is an important consideration for us in this text since it was only with the creation of economic surplus that an extensive system of social stratification came into being. Inequality in the distribution of the goods and services of a society first appeared on a large scale during the Bronze Age, when the more powerful group members began to use their strength to obtain larger shares of

[10] Insightful analyses of the theories of Lenski, as well as the functionalists and conflict theorists, can be found in Duberman (1976) and Parenti (1978).

---

the surplus. With the emergence of private ownership and the related concept of inheritance, the way was opened for the development of a relatively permanent division of the society into social classes. As Bottomore notes, social classes "originated with the first historical expansion of productive forces beyond the level needed for mere subsistence, involving the extension of the division of labor outside the family, the accumulation of surplus wealth, and the emergence of private ownership of economic resources" (1978; p. 15).

Although not considered to be a Marxist sociologist, Lenski argued that **privilege,** or control over a portion of the surplus wealth, has its basis in power. Prestige, or one's esteem in the eyes of others, is a function of both power (that which enables a person to claim privilege) and privilege (actual possession of resources or rewards, such as income, wealth, land, and so forth). These concepts are relevant to the present analysis of age and stratification for, if we want to understand the position of old people in contemporary society, it is necessary that we investigate the sources of power that old people possess, the mechanisms by which this power is converted into privilege, and the role of both power and privilege in determining the prestige (or status) ascribed to old people as a group.

However, in order to proceed in this direction, we must move beyond Lenski's analysis, since it is incomplete in several important areas. First and most important, although Lenski uses the term *power* throughout his discussion, he never makes clear how people gain or exercise this precious commodity. Second, as Lenski himself points out, his theory predicts that the greatest inequality among social classes will be found in modern industrial societies —a prediction clearly not confirmed by empirical evidence. It is Lenski's ambiguous use of the term *power,* however, that is most problematic for the present analysis. How do people "get" power and, once obtained, how does power beget privilege and prestige? The answers to these questions have long preoccupied stratification theorists, and it is not likely that the answers offered here will prevent continued analysis. However, I believe that these questions, particularly the question how one acquires power, can be answered through application of the concepts of *dependence* and *deference.* The dependence variable will be discussed in greater detail in the next chapter, so let it suffice to say here that power is acquired through the ability to satisfy one's needs without having to depend upon or become indebted to other people. The reader may recognize this as a central assumption underlying the exchange theories of Emerson (1962) and Blau (1964a).

The concept of *deference* may help in answering the question of how power is used to acquire privilege and prestige. Shils (1975) refers to deference as the tendency for a social actor to "appreciate" or "derogate" the partner with whom social interaction occurs. In face-to-face interaction, deference is "often but not always accorded primarily with respect to status in the larger society" (Shils, 1975, p. 277). Shil's use of the term *deference* is consistent with exchange theorists' use of the word *power;* that is, both terms are used in connection with social interaction, rather than with single individuals. A person's privilege and prestige, for example, does not come automatically from power or "the possession of certain entitlements" but is instead "an element in a relationship between the person deferred to and the deferent person" (Shils, 1975, p. 287). Without social interaction, the power of an individual cannot be translated into privilege or prestige. Indeed, power itself cannot be conceptualized apart from the interaction of at least two people. So, to suggest that a person or group of people (say, the aged) lacks power is to suggest that, with respect to a second individual or group (for example, the middle-aged), the person or group generally is deferent and, therefore, subordinate.

One may question Shils' assertion that *all* social interaction involves deference, since so many of the daily encounters among people seem fairly routinized and not at all like the drama suggested by the phrase "acts of appreciation and derogation." Deference is present nonetheless, according to Shils. It is readily apparent, for instance, when the aged widow accedes to her child's suggestion that she enter a nursing home. It is present as well, however, in the *routine* conversation between members of different generations. Indeed, deference never is totally absent from any of our conversations or encounters with others in our social world. In other words, although it may not be recognized in every act or utterance, it is always there, near the surface, ready to be shown at the appropriate time. Deference is, as Shils notes, sometimes concentrated (evident) and sometimes not. When not concentrated, deference "survives in attenuation, in a pervasive, intangible form that enters into all sorts of relationships through tone of speech, demeanor, precedence in speaking, frequency and mode of contradiction, and so forth (1975, p. 288–289).

Whether one receives or shows deference, which generally is directed upward from lower-status to higher-status individuals, depends on the relative positions of the social actors involved. This fact underlies many of the transition problems faced by older persons upon retirement, the death of a spouse, relocation to a nursing home, or other similar life changes. The routine showing of deference brings with it a degree of predictability to social relations that most people find satisfying, and it also gives an indication of how the actors view themselves and their status relative to other people. When one of the actors involved undergoes a transition in his or her *social* identity (a worker becomes a retiree, for example), deference relationships must be renegotiated to reflect the shift in power. Shils goes so far as to suggest that deference may even become *extinct*. If a person loses power, Shils argues that, "in the course of time," the person will also lose the deference that the power (Shils uses the term entitlements) brought him or her.

An individual's power is derived from the ability to satisfy perceived needs or to achieve goals with a minimum amount of dependence upon other persons. In satisfying perceived needs, the individual accumulates *privilege,* or a share of a society's surplus (Lenski, 1966): the resources that enable the person to remain independent—that is, not dependent upon the resources of another person are also used as credit that the person uses to claim a "legitimate" share of the group's goods. Privilege is then converted into prestige during social interaction. In this process, deference is the link between privilege and prestige; it is manifested through conversation and other communication media, and it serves to signal any change in the relative power structure among the participants.

Before we move on to a discussion of the relationship of power, stratification, and the aged, two additional points must be made concerning the relationship between power and privilege. First, the relationship is reciprocal; that is, although power is the basis of privilege, an increase in privilege serves to increase power as well (see Figure 2–2). For example, an increase in wealth is a goal that may be reached by the use of power. On the one hand, therefore, an increase in wealth increases privilege, on the other hand, however, an increase in wealth also increases the actor's independence, or power.

The second point concerns the basis of power, about which Lenski unfortunately says very little. I have already suggested that power involves independence or autonomy, but independence itself is relative; it is not a constant characteristic of individuals. To say that a person has power is to say that, in the process of achieving a goal, he or she has remained relatively independent of other people. But how does an actor remain relatively independent? The answer is through *resources*. Through the possession of objects, traits, or qualities defined by a group as desirable (and, therefore, desired), the individual is able to exert power in a social relationship.

Resources can be classified into five categories:

1. *Personal Characteristics,* such as strength, beauty, charm, integrity, courage, intelligence, knowledge, and so forth;
2. *Material Possessions,* such as money or property;
3. *Relational Characteristics,* such as influential friends or relatives or caring children;
4. *Authority,* such as that associated with political office, position in a formal organization, or status within a group (such as the status of parent in the family);
5. *Generalized Reinforcers,* such as respect, approval, recognition, support, and other rewards.

POWER ⟶ PRIVILEGE ⟶ PRESTIGE
(Deference)

FIGURE 2–2.   *The reciprocal relationship between power and privilege*

Of these five types of power resources, *material possessions* is the category that is also an aspect of *privilege*. We all know that money can be used to make more money; so, money can be defined as both a resource of power and an aspect of privilege. More will be said on the subject of power resources in the next chapter.

Power, Stratification, and Old People

The system of age stratification, because it involves "class," is also a system in which power is exercised. Age cohorts, although they don't constitute social classes according to most definitions, have certain elements in common with social classes. Most important to the present analysis, privilege and prestige are found in unequal measure among different age groups, just as they are among different social classes. Since the surplus of a society is inherently limited, and since the distribution of a surplus is based on power, age relations are power relations. The relationship between a retired worker and his or her middle-aged landlord, for example, is a power relationship. So, too, is the relationship between a widow and her middle-aged daughter. All that is meant by the term *power relationship* is that the social interaction between two individuals or groups involves the exchange of power resources. Thus, the greater the number and/or quality (desirability) of resources, the more power the individual is able to exercise.

Old people in modern society, because of their exclusion from labor markets, are disadvantaged in their intergenerational relations. Of the five types of resources, material possessions, particularly money, are the most widely accepted and easily transferred. Since the principal means by which most people acquire money is participation in labor markets, old people are limited in their access to material possessions as well as their access to positions of authority, since they are not usually active in the labor market. In old age, it is often necessary to rely upon those possessions previously accumulated, because material resources rarely accrue significantly after occupational retirement.

Old people are further disadvantaged in intergenerational relations, because their access to other power resources, including both personal and relational characteristics, is also limited. For example, aging brings with it a decline in strength and beauty (as generally defined); thus, these two power resources become inaccessible for the aged. Beauty is, of course, in the eye of the beholder; yet, physical beauty is generally associated with youth, not old age. This is not to suggest that old people lack beauty. Indeed, in the interaction among old people, beauty again becomes a power resource, because some old people are certainly more beautiful than others. It is in cross-age interaction that the aged usually cannot rely on beauty as a power resource. This difference serves to illustrate how power is relative (cf., Lehman, 1977): the value of a power resource such as beauty is greatest when the resource is combined with other resources, such as money. The value of being wealthy *and* attractive is obvious; the liquidity of beauty without wealth, however, is limited. The fact that power is relative suggests that those who view power as inevitably linked with *force*—for example, Bierstedt (1950, p. 202), who suggests that "power is latent force"—are defining the concept in an unnecessarily restrictive way.

Another illustration of the relativity of power is the increasing probability that death will steal from aging people the friends and relatives who serve as important sources of power. In fact, the only major source of power left untouched by the aging process is the category of generalized reinforcers. Yet, since respect or approval are universally available, they are also less valued than other types of power resources. In any case, the mere fact that aging does not *decrease* one's access to power resources does not constitute an advantage; aging does not *increase* one's access to them either.

When one considers how power resources for old people dwindle, it is somewhat incongruous to read stratification theorists' accounts of old age. Lenski (1966) and Abrams (1970), for example, claim that aging brings *increased,* not fewer, resources. Their apparent disregard of the fact that most old people are not members of the ruling elite is suggested by the following quote:

> The key fact with respect to age stratification in all advanced industrial societies is the economic, political, and general organizational dominance of the older segments of the population [1966, p. 406].

Lenski goes on to list the average ages of United States senators, American military leaders, members of the property and managerial elites, and others. Such an analysis makes a serious error by both confusing the middle-aged with the aged and analyzing the distribution of resources by age only for the dominant classes (ruling elites) and not for the working classes. Lenski shows how age favors the old within a small proportion of the population. Certainly among the majority of the lower and working classes (to which almost half of all Americans belong),[11] resources do *not* increase past middle age.

Although some argue that resources are greatest among the older segments of the population, others insist that, although resources do decline in old age, the decline is not particularly problematic. This is the fallacy of the argument called *The Old Need Less*. An example of this argument is the observation that most old people seem quite able to get along with reduced

---

[11] The numbers of working-class and middle-class citizens may be calculated in a variety of ways, thus leading to some confusion over the relative size of each class. Our estimate of "almost half" (48%) is taken from Giddens (1973). Levison (1975) estimates that, if only males were considered, the working class would actually be larger than the middle class (57% to 42%).

income. They are probably able to make do, according to some, because of disengagement. Streib (1976, p. 164), for example, argues that the "elderly often voluntarily curtail their needs, activities, and consumption patterns in accord with their declining energy, declining interests, and declining income." In addition, Streib states that "a person with an older self-image may manage comfortably on a smaller income because he has 'disengaged from consumerism,' so to speak." The notion of a voluntary curtailment of lifestyle, however, is speculation—a conclusion with no basis in evidence. The only conclusion from Streib's observations that appears warranted is that when the income of a group is reduced, people make do with less income. What other choice does a person have? If one excludes suicide, theft, or loans, there remains little to do when a person's income is reduced but struggle to make do. To suggest this is voluntary is beside the point; it is, for most old people, the *only* viable option.

The argument of disengagement theorists that old people voluntarily disengage in order to prepare for death and attain the new "equilibrium" characteristic of "successful aging" simply has no factual basis. Although aspects of the disengagement theory do retain significance for current work in aging, the voluntary-withdrawal notion is not one of them. Thus, for some, it may be "one of the paradoxes in later life . . . that persons can suffer severe declines in income, yet still retain essentially the same style of life" (Streib, 1976, p. 165). For others, however, including the present writer, there is no paradox: old age is associated with a decline in resources that serves to drastically alter the old person's social interactions and self-concept.[12] If "style of life" refers to the tendency of many old people to live in their homes for as long as possible, then it is true that style of life is unchanged. Yet, if one considers the change in the number and quality of old people's social interactions (as well as the fact that their house still requires maintenance and takes up a greater part of their income), one realizes that the style of life *changes* in old age (cf. Alberoni, 1971). Thus, there is no paradox.

The aged are, in fact, similar to the unemployed, the destitute, and others in the subordinate classes of industrial societies in that they are the people who "get least of what there is to get" (Miliband, 1969, quoted in Parenti, 1978). The lack of resources available to old people is described in the following passage:

> Class position becomes an important factor in shaping the life conditions of the elderly. Like the very young, the very old suffer from natural disabilities when attempting to compete for social outputs. In a society that places a premium on beauty, youth, energy, speed, earning power, aggressive drive, and productivity, the old and infirm are easily deprived of their place in the sun. When one's status and security is determined by one's ability either to control wealth or

[12] For an excellent article suggesting an interesting application of disengegement theory, see Streib (1968).

sell one's labor on the market, the superannuated are a surplus people of little use to the productive system, to their families and, as often happens, to themselves. The deference accorded a person of years in more traditional societies is replaced with impatience, patronization, neglect, and finally incarceration in a nursing home. As the elderly are given more years to live, they are given less reason to live [Parenti, 1978, p. 68].

Other sources of power, in addition to money, that are unequally distributed among age groups are *time* and *charisma*. These are *personal* characteristics that tend to favor the young. I say "tend" to favor the young since the relationship between age and charisma—although not the relationship between age and time, which always favors the young, varies by level of societal modernization. Time is, of course, a precious resource because it is nonreplaceble and finite. Young people, more so than old people, have time "on their side." Time, in this sense, may be difficult to employ as a power resource in any single or nonreoccurring situation. However, in the long run, young people generally outlast the aged and, therefore, can strike a tougher bargain in their intergenerational relationships.

In particular, charisma tends to favor the young in industrial, or modern, societies. For example, the heroes of our popular culture, whether in music, athletics, or politics, are, almost without exception, young, In Shils' (1975) terms, charisma adheres to those closest to the "center" of society; the center reflects a society's core values, those that "legitimate or withhold legitimacy from the earthly powers or that dominate earthly existence" (Shils, 1975, p. 279).

Although in contemporary society, charisma attaches more readily to youthful persons than to old, this is not true of other societies or other times. In times past, when the center of a society was dominated by religion, superstition, or magic, the aged were viewed as having a great deal of charisma because of their control over the exercise of rituals, their knowledge of the past and magical things, and their closeness to death and, therefore, to the deities (cf. Goody, 1976). Among the Kiwai Papuans, for example, children stood in awe of old people because of their magical powers. Landtman (1938) describes Papuan youth crouching in a stooped position when passing a group of elders, since boys were "afraid of rousing the angry attention of some elder who could easily harm (them) by means of sorcery at the slightest cause of displeasure" (p. 21). Also, charisma as a characteristic of old people is generally found in predominantly agrarian societies. Among the Yahgan of Tierra del Fuego, to cite another example, it is reported that "almost every elderly man is said to be a wizard" (Landtman, 1938, p. 143).

In modern society, the supernatural plays a peripheral, rather than central, role. The roles that do have authority and control society—and that, therefore, represent the center of modern life—are the secular positions of judge, governor, scientist, and technocrat. The charisma of the aged in modern society, as a result, is diminished to almost nothing, save for the exceptional few who, like George Meany, Bertrand Russell, or Pablo Casals, were able to maintain a valuable skill or office.

The Persistence of Stratification Hierarchies: The Problem of Legitimation

Stratification on the basis of age, like methods of distributing the excess goods of a society, persists because those who suffer or derive only minimum benefits from the system either accept it as legitimate or are powerless to change it. Obviously, those who benefit most from any institutional arrangement are mostly likely to prefer maintenance of the status quo.

Old people have, for the most part, accepted their subordinate position in the age-stratification system. There have been occasional indications of organized anger on the part of the aged, such as the Townsend Movement during the 1930s, the McLain Movement following World War II, and, most recently, the Gray Panthers. Most studies indicate, however, that the number of old people who are "age conscious" remains relatively small (Dowd, 1978b). The reasons for this are similar to the reasons why many workers are decidedly not class conscious. First, the aged are relatively unorganized and, as a consequence, powerless when pitted against the myriad laws and policies that mandate age as a legal basis of discrimination and exclusion. Second, many old people have internalized and accepted as legitimate the continued use of age as a criterion for stratification. Like the young, old people tend to prefer what is familiar, and they fear and dislike the unknown or uncertain. (Studies, for example, on the attitudinal effect of "mere exposure" to certain words and categories of objects demonstrate that subjects consistently demonstrate a preference for those words that appear frequently in common usage.)[13] Third, many people tend to view existing institutional structures as just and appropriate. The accumulated "tradition" of existing structures renders them very resistent to change. This fact is recognized by politicans as part of the advantage of the incumbent in an election.

In the case of retirement policies, many people—including the aged —if they ever think about the matter at all, tend to take for granted that retirement will occur at a specified age. These policies have been in existence long enough to be almost invisible. Like sexism prior to the women's liberation movement, ageism is an unconscious ideology. Forced retirement and other manifestations of age stratification have been institutionalized in our society and have become, with time, legitimated; they are examples of our tendency to perceive what "is" as what, therefore, "has to be."

[13] The social psychologist Zajonc is most closely associated with the "mere exposure" literature. See, for example, Zajonc (1968).

At this point in the text, I want to point out that, in spite of one's dissatisfaction with society's callous treatment of many old people, in order to analyze stratification one must recognize that no system of distribution will ever eliminate inequality within a society. This is, as Dahrendorf cogently argues, the dynamic element of history. There will always be conflict among groups in capitalist economies for a greater share of society's surplus. Regardless of the morality of such behavior, all members of a class or stratum "have a vested interest in protecting or increasing the value of their common resources and in reducing the value of competitive resources that constitute the bases of other classes" (Lenski, 1966, p. 76). This applies to the aged no less than to other groups within society. The reluctance of old people in preindustrialized societies to share their "privilege" with younger age groups supports the proposition that to possess power is to use it.

One mechanism for protecting resources and power, which I shall discuss in more detail in later chapters, is *ideology*—a system of beliefs that supports the dominant class by legitimating its exploitation of subordinate groups. It is apparent that any effort to effect a redistribution of societal resources must first identify the society's ideologies and demonstrate their pervasive effect, because such legitimating myths—what Weber calls *status-legends*—serve to maintain the conditions that allow continued operation of existing institutional arrangements. In capitalist society, the ideology of private control of free enterprise serves the interests of the business and political elites who reap the major profits from the system. So, too, the "myth of the Golden Years" (Gubrium, 1973), which posits a notion of successful aging that includes retirement from active participation in labor markets, serves the interests of younger age groups. This is another example of the ironic tendency of those groups who benefit least from existing structures to become some of the staunchest supporters of the structures. Although belying the market assumption of rational behavior, this tendency does suggest that dominant groups in capitalist societies have been very successful in achieving a major goal of dominant groups everywhere—the ability to keep others subordinate without using overt coercion (Collins, 1975). As Rousseau (as quoted in Parenti, 1978, p. 83) observed in the *Social Contract:* the "strongest is never strong enough to be always master, unless he transforms his strength into right and obedience into duty."

Review Questions

1. Contrast psychoanalytic and functionalist theories of generational relations.
2. Define social stratification.
3. What is "privilege" and how does it depend on the production of an economic surplus?

4. What are the five categories of power resources? Are the possession of power resources related to aging in any way?
5. Social interaction involves an exercise of deference. Explain.
6. How are age strata and social classes similar?
7. What are some of the problems involved in assigning old people to a particular social class?
8. What are the three effects designated by the acronym APC? Discuss the differences among these effects.
9. What is the "old need less" fallacy?

3

Power,
Dependency, and
Old Age

The key to systems of stratification, including both age and class systems, is power. As I indicated in the preceding chapter, much of the difficulty in dealing with the "overlaps" among stratification hierarchies has resulted from a tendency of theorists to *reify* these structures—that is, to think of them as having meaning or existence apart from the social interaction of the people who comprise them. The value of an exchange view of stratification systems is that it requires an integration of the social-structural and individual levels of analysis. Specifically, exchange theory breathes life into stratification theory by introducing social interaction as the bridge between social structure and the individual; exchange theory also sensitizes the observer to the critical role of power and power resources in determining the course of everyday social life. In this chapter, I will discuss the central components of exchange theory—including power, **dependency,** and exchange rates—and demonstrate the usefulness of such an approach to the study of aging.[1]

Social Structure, Power, and Exchange

Social structures, such as class hierarchies, are both real and imagined. Although they certainly have real effects on one's chances for success in life and one's access to various opportunities for social interaction, they do not exist independently; they exist only through the interaction of people. Although some Marxist writers, notably Lukács, tend to present classes as "acting subjects" who execute various defined "historical tasks" (Giddens, 1973), such a view overlooks the heterogeneity of experience contained within a particular social class. There is no organization or entity known as The Working Class. There are only workers. To analyze social structures, then, we must occasionally make reference to individuals and their social interactions.

All social interaction may be viewed as an exchange of rewarding behaviors between two social actors—be they individuals or larger units such as corporations or nation-states. In the terms of behavioral psychology, it is "an interactive relation between two parties . . . based upon reciprocal reinforcement" (Stolte & Emerson, 1977, p. 119). Human behavior tends to be oriented toward the expectations of other people; it also is motivated by a desire to maximize one's rewards and to minimize one's costs. People tend to avoid the undesirable and to seek pleasure or rewards.

Social interaction is the principal medium for exchanging activities and sentiments. Because social interaction involves individuals, it is individuals who constitute the major source of both our rewards and our costs. Although rewards certainly include money and other material things, rewards are also obtained through social interaction; thus, rewards may include "help in solving a problem . . . the transmission of technical information, the expression of affection, labor at a machine, or payment of money" (Stolte & Emerson, 1977, p. 119).

---

[1] Within the last several years, increasing numbers of sociologists incorporated concepts from exchange theory into their research on old people. Although, as yet, there has not appeared a sufficient number of books and articles on aging written from an exchange perspective to warrant its elevation to a position alongside the dominant role-theory paradigm, exchange theory does appear to have gained a foothold within the discipline of social gerontology. For an overview of several exchange applications see: Arling, Parham, & Teitelman (1978); Bengtson and Dowd (in press); Christoffersen (1974); Dowd (1975a, b); Dowd and LaRossa (1978); Fairchild, Pruchno, & Kahana, (1978); Gilford (1978); Gilford and Bengtson (1977); Johnson and Kamara (1977); Maddox and Wiley (1976); Rosenmayr (1974); Streib and Streib (1978); and Sussman (1975, 1976).

As one begins to view social interaction as primarily an exchange of resources, two questions come to mind: (1) What constitutes a reasonable, or satisfactory, exchange? (2) How do individuals, who may be strangers to each other, decide the basis and rules for the exchange? It is in answering these questions that the intricate relationship between social structure and individual behavior becomes apparent. As people interact with each other, they set precedents. Each interaction serves as a basis for conducting and evaluating future encounters of the same or similar type. As Collins perceptively notes, "men live by anticipating future encounters and remembering past ones" (1975). After repeated instances of social interaction in which the same or similar individuals exchange the same or similar behaviors (rewards), the interaction pattern may be termed *routinized* or *institutionalized;* that is, the pattern has been sufficiently established for individuals to know and expect a certain reward for a certain behavior. Indeed, this is what we mean when we refer to "social structure": it is the regularization or routinization of social interaction. Social exchange thus supports existing systems of stratification by creating—through the differentiation of power and dependence—super-ordinate and subordinate relationships (Mitchell, 1978).

Just as social structure has its basis in social interaction, social interaction is in turn determined to a large degree by the ranking of the exchange partners in the social structure. In other words, social class affects social exchange. The answer to each of the two questions raised in the preceding paragraph can be traced directly to this reciprocal relationship. Reasonable exchange is what individuals come to accept as reasonable, based upon previous experience in a similar situation (or knowledge of others in similar situations). Exchange rules come into being through negotiation among social actors, each of whom has a certain amount of **power resources.** The nature and degree of power resources held by an individual are affected by the individual's class position, as well as by the culture-influenced evaluations of such "status characteristics" as race, sex, and, of course, age! An individual's sense of efficacy—the determinant of performance or "presentation of self" (Goffman, 1959) in exchange interactions—is in turn affected by the exchange value of his or her power resources. In order to realize maximum "profit" from a social exchange, the individual's presentation of self must be convincing. Indeed, on certain occasions, individuals receive greater rewards than normally expected (for example, the classic case of the parvenu). However, on the average, one's profit is positively associated with one's investment of resources, which is itself a function of class membership or social status.

The showing of deference is similarly affected by class membership. Recall from Figure 2-2 that deference is the aspect of social interaction that involves derogation or appreciation and that links power and privilege with prestige. Although exchange rates are determined by the relative power of the actors, they are negotiated in social interaction through the granting or denial of deference. In a sense, the role of deference is to communicate the status rankings of exchange partners to each other (as well as to the interested observer). Collins notes, for example, that the social-class memberships of individuals may be reconstructed from observing deference relations:

> On this basis, three main classes can be distinguished: those who take orders from few or none but give orders to many; those who must defer to some people but can command others; and those who are order-takers only [1975, p. 63].[2]

The effect of social structure on social exchange is most clearly evident when the social actors occupy different positions in a particular stratification hierarchy—for example, the positions of middle-aged child and aged parent. Since the resources of the actors are unequal, the rules for the exchange (how much babysitting is expected for a weekly visit?) are decided by the actor with the greatest resources. The actor with the greatest power is able to dictate the terms of the exchange.[3] The routinization of this type of exchange creates several problems for the subordinate party. The immediate danger is that, over time, "unfair" exchange rates become "fair" exchange rates (Martin, 1971). The emergence of mandatory retirement policies during the rapid industrialization of our economy before World War I is an example of the institutionalization of an unbalanced exchange rate that later provided the normative basis for routine exchanges.

To summarize this section on social structure and social exchange, I would say that social interaction is essentially a process of social exchange that both modifies social structure through routinized exchange rates and is itself affected by structural factors in the guise of social class and other status factors. Also, I would add that exchange relations have three general components:

1. a *psychological* component—the existence of human needs (both basic needs and socially created needs)
2. a *social psychological* component—the satisfaction of needs through social interaction in which behaviors are reciprocated
3. a *sociological* component—the negotiation of exchange rates as a function of power resources, which are positively associated with social class

---

[2] This and all other quotations from this source are from *Conflict Sociology: Toward an Explanatory Science*, by R. Collins. Copyright 1975 by Academic Press, Inc. Reprinted by permission of the author and publisher.

[3] Recent "conflict analysis" of social-interaction processes also emphasizes the role of power in determining outcomes. Although the conflict approach is presumably more "structural" and thus refrains from using the language of exchange theory, when applied to interaction processes the two approaches are remarkably similar. Hajda recognizes this parallel development as he observes (1977, p. 2): "If conflict theory . . . has a natural ally, it is the exchange theory . . . " See, also, Archibald (1976) or, for an "energy theory" approach to the issues, Adams (1975).

Power and Dependence in Social Exchange

The most recent developments in the theory of exchange have been elaborations of the role of *power* in exchange. This research is particularly exciting to sociologists in the field of aging, because it brings the opportunity to integrate a large number of empirical findings within a single theoretical framework. A major contributor to this literature since the early 1960s has been Richard M. Emerson. Emerson's first breakthrough was his demonstration that social exchange is a function of the relative power (and inversely, the relative dependence) of the actors involved.

In Emerson's view, power is derived from an *imbalance* in a social-exchange relationship. Exchange relations are said to be balanced if the profits gained by each exchange partner are comparable. Profits are defined as rewards minus costs, and costs refer either to the "difficulties" experienced in an exchange relation (an "obnoxious" exchange partner, for example[4]) or to the rewards forfeited by choosing one particular course of action. If people place great value on the rewards they receive from exchange partners, they must be willing and able to reciprocate with a behavior or resource that will compensate the partners for the resources they gave up. If they are unable to reciprocate in kind, the relationships may dissolve; however, if there are no alternative relationships to depend on to supply the rewards given up by dissolving the first relationship, dissolution may be unacceptable. In such a case, an actor may be required by his or her exchange partner to lower the profits by either accepting fewer rewards from the partner or incurring greater costs by giving up more resources to the partner. In any case, *imbalance* means that one actor, Actor *A*, becomes *dependent* upon the exchange partner, since the reward supplied by the partner is both valued and unavailable elsewhere at similar levels of profit, and that Actor *B* has *power* over Actor *A*. Power is, in effect, a relative characteristic; it depends on the relationship of Actor *A* and Actor *B*.

Emerson's contribution to exchange theory has been the recognition that power and dependence are opposite sides of the same exchange relation. He demonstrated these concepts as follows:

    a. *Power:* "In any exchange relation A_x ; B_y (when *A* and *B* represent the actors, and *x* and *y* the resources involved in the exchange and x/y the exchange ratio), the *power* of *A* over *B* (P_{AB}) is the ability of *A* to decrease the ratio x/y."

    b. *Power Advantage:* "The power advantage of one actor over another is equivalent to the power differential between *A* and *B* (or $P_{AB} - P_{BA}$)."

    c. *Dependence:* "The dependence of *A* on B_j (D_{AB_j}) is a joint function 1) varying directly with the value to *A* of resources received from B_j and

---

[4] For a recent discussion of "obnoxious" social actors, see Davis and Schmidt (1977).

2) varying inversely with the comparison level for alternative exchange relations"[5] [1972, p. 67].

Aspects of Emerson's theory on power and dependence in exchange relations have been independently developed by other researchers. For example, there is the idea of "comparison levels for alternatives," borrowed from the work of Thibaut and Kelley (1959) and Kelley and Thibaut (1978). The comparison level for alternative exchange relations refers to the number of alternative exchange relations A has with C, D, and other partners possessing resources similar to B's (Stolte & Emerson, 1977, p. 120). When a person interacts with another, according to Thibaut and Kelly, "he compares and evaluates his outcome in the relationship with the best possible outcome that he can expect in alternative relationships. This expected outcome in alternative relationships is called his 'comparison level for alternatives' . . . " (Komorita, 1977, p. 69).

Dependency, like power, is always relative—it cannot be assessed as an absolute quantity (Mennell, 1974). This relational aspect of power and dependency is not merely an academic distinction; it has profound implications for social policy concerning the aged. Some research has taken the position that dependency is a characteristic of individuals. The implication inherent in such a view is that, if dependency is considered problematic and something that should be corrected, remedial action takes the form of individual "rehabilitation" or self-help. Such a policy is bound for failure since it would ignore the exchange partner and the balance of power in the relationship. Jacobsen is incorrect in his assertion that "dependency is a condition; . . . you are either in or out of a state of dependency" (1978, p. 4). Such a view ignores the fact that, in order to eliminate dependency, each individual's relationship with others in his or her social world must change. Neither of the strategies to eliminate dependency recommended by Jacobsen would have a significant impact; in fact, they would probably increase dependency. Jacobsen's first recommendation that, for certain dependent individuals, "self-help and individual effort will be the major restorative strategy," will not solve the problem. Although this recommendation must certainly please cost-conscious officials of service bureaucracies, it will do little to change the balance of exchange relationships, because it does nothing to increase the dependent person's supply of power resources.

Jacobsen's second recommendation suggests that family and community-based agencies be used to deal with dependency. Jacobsen suggests, for example, that we investigate "incentives for caregiving by family and friends" (1978, p. 12).[6] This particular strategy is problematic for several reasons; for

---

[5] These quotes can also be found in an interesting application of exchange theory to interorganizational relations by Cook (1977). Other applications of exchange theory to formal organizations include Jacobs (1974) and Stinchcombe (1970).

[6] I use Jacobsen only to illustrate the general view of dependence as a psychological, or individual, characteristic. Others who share this view include Paillot (1976); Shanan and Weihl (1976); and Solem (1976). A good overview of the general issues surrounding dependency in old age may be found in Van den Heuvel (1976).

example, many people resent the intrusion of government into the area of primary group relations, and, even if incentives can be identified that encourage family members and friends to give "care" to the old person, the net effect of such a one-way nonreciprocal exchange of resources would be to *increase* the old person's dependency. For this reason, the alternative proposal of Sussman (1976) that monetary incentives for reintegrating old people into families be funneled through the old people themselves holds considerably greater promise of success. I will return to these issues in Chapter Six.

Status Characteristics and Exchange

As we have seen, one major development in the literature on exchange theory was Emerson's work on power/dependence relations. A second major development involves the expansion of our knowledge of how status characteristics affect exchange processes. Status characteristics are important in social exchange because they constitute "a characteristic around which differences in cognitions and evaluations of individuals . . . come to be organized" (Berger, Fisek, Norman, & Zelditch, 1977, p. 3). This suggests that any status characteristic of an individual, such as the person's age or sex, may become a factor in the negotiation of exchange rates. Although people may know little about their exchange partners, other than the obvious visible characteristics of age, race, sex, and perhaps, class, social interaction will probably be organized around common meanings associated with these status characteristics. Age, for example, is an "exportable" characteristic—one which accompanies the person and enters into the process of evaluating whether the person's claim for a certain level of reward is legitimate. The meaning and value attributed to status characteristics are not, of course, immanent in the characteristic itself, but are defined in the interaction process (Berger & Fisek, 1970). Thus, the value attributable to age and, hence, the value of age as a power resource, varies from culture to culture and from one historical era to another. The historical variability of age status will constitute the focus of Chapter Four.

Status characteristics frequently have insidious effects, because they tend to influence others' perceptions of us in areas that presumably have no connection with these characteristics. For example, without knowing anything about an old person's strength, we presume it to be minimal. And, knowing nothing about an old person's intelligence, many people presume that it is low. Webster and Driskell (1978) call this phenomenon *status generalization,* which refers to "the process by which statuses of actors external to a particular interaction are imported and allowed to determine important features of that interaction" (p. 220).

Even though this process may not always be conscious, its effects on the social actor with the devalued status characteristic (old age, for example)

---

weaken his or her bargaining position in the negotiation of a favorable exchange rate. Exchange partners tend to place "the burden of proof" on old people to demonstrate that their investments (and, therefore, the legitimacy of their claims for certain rewards) should not be discounted simply because they happen to possess the status characteristic of old age. Webster and Driskell elaborate the "burden of proof" idea:

> The burden of proof principle states that, unless the relevance or applicability of an external status characteristic is challenged, actors will *infer* task-specific performance expectations on the basis of any discriminable status characteristic they possess. Such inferences occur regardless of the actual relevance of the status characteristic to the task at hand. In other words, individuals act as if the burden of proof is placed upon demonstrating that the status characteristic is not relevant rather than demonstrating that it *is* relevant to the task at hand" [1978, p. 222].

The aged are in a *double* bind, then, in their social-exchange relationships. On the one hand, access to several categories of exchange resources tends to decline with age, thus placing the old person in a weak negotiating position.[7] On the other hand, the resources that the old person does possess are perceived as *less* valuable because of the "burden of proof" principle; that is, the *value* of an exchange resource—when possessed by an aged actor—is not self-evident. Because of the actor's age, the value or the resource must be demonstrated!

The Use of Power in Social Exchange

In discussing with students or colleagues the power element in relationships between old people and their adult children, I occasionally hear the disclaimer that although, in general, power struggles may underlie intergenerational relations, they do not affect one's own cross-age contacts. However, such disclaimers involve the mistaken idea that, where love is present, power is not, and, conversely, where the use of power is evident, a feeling of primary group ties between the actors must be missing. Although it is true that an exchange-theory approach to interaction is more readily adapted to secondary relationships,[8] relations among family members and friends are also grist for the exchange-theory mill.[9]

---

[7] Komorita (1977) presents a nice discussion of the advantages inherent in "negotiating from strength."

[8] The well-known example of the co-workers in a service bureaucracy, given by Blau (1964) and repeated by Homans (1974) and others, illustrates the utility of exchange concepts in analyses of secondary relations.

[9] The decision to have children, for example, depends on the distribution of power resources within the marital dyad. For an interesting analysis of power and exchange among married couples, see LaRossa (1977).

Most conflict and exchange theorists agree that to have power is to use it. Goode notes that we all use whatever power we have to achieve desired outcomes:

> Everyone learns, consciously or not, accurately or not, various ways of controlling others for one's own ends. Few people spend much time calculating how to control others but everyone does so part of the time [1972, p. 507].

In effect, the use of power is inevitable, for "whatever we do has some effect on others, to our advantage or not, in conformity with our wishes or not, and whether or not we will it so" (Goode, 1972, p. 507).

Although power is present in all social interaction, that does not mean that every *individual* uses power in each and every interaction. The unit of analysis is the interaction, not the individual. When individuals interact, the negotiation of the exchange rate may occur without a show of force, a baring of teeth, or even a verbal discussion of each other's claims. Frequently, the exchange rate is determined merely by an inspection of the visible status characteristics of the exchange partner, followed by an evaluation and relative ranking of these characteristics vis-à-vis one's own. For example, in laboratory experiments, a male may presume to lead a group discussion, and a woman may tacitly concur by relating to him as a leader. The *use* of power, in this case, is invisible. Its effect on exchange may be due simply to the actors' shared understanding of the value (and therefore power) associated with a particular combination of status characteristics.

Gamson disagrees with this explanation of the use of power in social exchange, and he argues in *Power and Discontent* (1968) that power is not to be confused with influence. Gamson believes that "there are many reasons why even someone with an abundance of resources may not exercise influence on a given decision." He lists, as examples, a person's indifference to a particular outcome; a limitation of resources; the possibility of incurring greater costs; or the relatively greater resources of the other actor. Gamson's analysis is appropriate; his conclusion, however, stems from an emphasis on the individuals rather than on the actual social exchange. In this way, he reduces power to an observable, individual behavior instead of seeing it as an agreement among social actors on the value of a particular resource, such as age or money. I would argue that power is always present in social interaction (except for mere passing encounters—for example, giving directions to a passerby) even if its only role is to preclude any overt demonstration of strength or force.

Although to have power is to use it, an interesting and often befuddling aspect of power/dependence relations is that to *use* power is eventually to *lose* power. To understand how this unlikely turn of events comes about, we need to imagine an exchange relation between two actors that continues over a period of time. We know that the exchange will involve power, with the partner possessing the power advantage using it to his or her advantage. Indeed, one can readily imagine a situation in which power is used to maximize profit, which increases the actor's power advantage, which, in turn, encourages the further use of power. This can be summarized as follows: "in any exchange relation $A_x: B_y$, if A has a power advantage, then A's use of power will increase across continuing transactions as a function of power advantage" (Cook, 1977, p. 67).

This proposition describes, however, only the short-term exchange relation. In the long run, the use of power by the partner with the advantage tends to *balance* the relative power of each partner. How does this work? In order to make sense of this apparent contradiction, one must recall Homans' assertion that social exchange will continue only so long as both partners find it profitable. Actually, by applying the concept CL_{ALT} (Comparison Level for Alternatives), one could argue that social exchange will continue only as long as the profits derived from the current relation are greater than the profits one could expect to receive from an alternative relation. Therefore, the mere fact that an actor, particularly the actor with the power advantage, remains involved in an exchange relation suggests that the relationship is one that provides the actor maximum profit.

From this, it follows that whatever resource is being supplied to the more powerful actor as part of a continuous exchange relation is perceived as rewarding. Indeed, the recipient probably is unable to obtain comparable levels of this reward at comparable cost anywhere. In effect, with the continuation of the interaction, the actor who was originally more powerful grows increasingly dependent on the reward. Therefore, it is not surprising why even the lowly resource of compliance is at times sufficient to balance an exchange ratio. After a continuous pattern of deferring to the wishes (or complying with the demands) of a more powerful exchange partner, a sudden withholding of this resource by the weaker partner may make it obvious to both how dependent the one actor has become. In this case, in order to continue receiving the same reward, the former will have to increase the size of the reward she or he is willing to exchange. In this way, exchange relations tend to become balanced over time.

Stated formally, this tendency toward balance may be expressed as follows: "In any exchange relation $A_x: B_y$, if A has a power advantage $D_{BA} > D_{AB}$ at time t_1, then D_{BA} decreases or D_{AB} increases across continuing transactions until $D_{AB} = D_{BA}$ at time t_n" (Emerson, 1972, p. 67).

Not all social exchange, however, becomes balanced with the passage of time. Some exchange relationships merely cease to continue. One case in point is the "disengagement" of some old people from society. In an earlier essay (Dowd, 1975a), I argued that disengagement, when it occurs, is probably a result of the decreasing power resources of old people relative to others in their environment. Continued engagement becomes too costly and, as a result, the perceived profits (or CL_{ALT}) of disengagement exceed the current minimal profits of engagement.

There is another aspect of the issue of dwindling power resources of the aged—an aspect that supports the disengagement theory's assertion that disengagement is a *mutual* withdrawal of the individual from society from the individual. Older people may elect to disengage when their costs increase to the point where profits diminish and withdrawal becomes a viable—indeed, in some cases, the only—option. Even if the old person attempts to remain "engaged" in social interaction, others are disengaging from the old person; although visits from family members continue, they are less frequent than before and probably shorter in duration.[10] Why should this be so? The first reason may be that visits are increasingly costly for the younger exchange partner. They take time away from other activities, and thus the individual incurs costs that may not be made up by the rewards. A second reason, which relates to our discussion of the use of power, is that people tend to curtail their interactions with the aged; otherwise, they run the risk of increasing *their* dependency on the aged. Such a dependency, given the possibility that the old person may soon die or become incapacitated, is perceived as potentially too costly. Mutual disengagement, then, is frequently the more profitable option for both partners.

Emerson's hypothesis that power imbalances tend to disappear over a period of repeated exchanges is not always supported by conflict theorists. Conflict theorists rightly point out that this hypothesis does not apply to strictly economic exchanges, like labor for wages. For example, Marx argued quite convincingly that such an "exchange" is really a non-exchange since the capitalist has to obtain more value than he has given. So, although the worker exchanges labor for a particular sum of money (wages), the capitalist gains the *use-value* of the worker's labor; that is, the capitalist is able to use the worker's labor to create a commodity whose ultimate worth is much greater than the wages paid to the worker (cf., Rosdolsky, 1977).

The historical record of labor-management negotiations supports the argument that the imbalance between workers and capitalists continues to favor the ruling class. Zeitlin notes that this particular exchange relation is very likely to continue, even given the obviously greater profits of management:

> The main source of this inherent imbalance is the fact that one party controls the means of production while the other does not; one party controls strategic resources and therefore commands, while the other party, if he is to gain his livelihood, must subordinate himself and obey [1973, p. 78]

Zeitlin raises an excellent point that requires elaboration: obviously, management controls greater resources than workers and derives greater rewards from the exchange, yet Zeitlin overlooks the many potential resources of workers when he suggests that workers *must* obey management. Workers do form unions and do on occasion withhold their labor from their employer

---

[10] Although the results of surveys suggest that old people see their children frequently (at least once a week), these results may be inaccurate since the social desirability of reporting frequent visits may lead some people to overestimate the frequency of contact. In any case, survey data tell us nothing about the "quality" of the interaction. It is questionable whether visits to an aging parent constitute a source of intimate contact for either party.

---

through strikes and work slow-downs. A good example of this is the case of professional athletes, particularly baseball players. The players' union, by challenging the legality of the so-called "reserve clause" in their contracts, won for the players the right to "free agency." Players may now auction their talents on the open market, a change that has had a dramatic impact on salaries. In addition, as the June 1968 strike by French workers suggests, the possibility remains that more workers will develop a class consciousness and, recognizing their collective power in the relationship, demand increased rewards from their employer.

It also must be recognized that, although a certain exchange relation may appear unfair to an observer, the participants may view it differently. For example, individual status characteristics play a major role in determining the rate at which rewards are distributed. Consequently, even though the actual rewards accruing to each partner may differ, most participants will view the exchange as legitimate as long as the profits are proportional to their "investments." Thus, the capitalists, and perhaps some workers as well, may argue that the capitalists' greater "investments" of social class, capital, or education, "justify" their claim to a proportionately larger share of rewards from the relationship.

It is only when profits and investments are not proportionate that the exchange may be said to be unfair. This fairness principle is known as the Rule of Distributive Justice.[11] It states that, as long as each party to the exchange receives profits proportional to investments, the exchange relation will continue. However, if power is used to attain a disproportionately large share of rewards, the probability increases that the oppressed (or subordinate) group will attempt to resist the unjust exercise of power through the development of an opposition ideology and, eventually, mobilization for change (Blau, 1964b, p.205). The work for change, of course, is directed at correcting the imbalance in the exchange relationship, and in this way it supports Homens' assertion that social exchange tends to continue only so long as the partners find it profitable.

In the area of exchange relations between the aged and the middle-aged as groups, the use of power over time could indeed lead to a state of balance. The aged possess the potential resource of sociopolitical organization and thus have the potential—even in modern industrial society—of enhancing their status relative to other age groups. What is required for such a movement, however, is the widespread recognition that age discrimination is illogical and unfair. However, until a large number of old people recognize that age discrimination is ill-founded, their relative status will remain low.

The development of age consciousness among old people, which I will discuss in greater detail in later chapters, is highly problematic because young

[11] Homans (1961; 1974) is generally credited with the sociological development of the concept of distributive justice, although it has a much longer history among moral philosophers. For a discussion of the historical context of the distributive justice rule, see Sidgwick (1966).

and old alike support, or at least accept, many current discriminatory practices, such as mandatory retirement. This is an excellent example of power being successfully transformed into legitimate authority; most people view such practices as being in the best interests of the country, not just the young. Thus, resentment and opposition have been effectively forestalled. The dominance of the middle-aged middle class persists, because this group is viewed by most people "not as a merely avaricious party seeking private ends, but as an agent of a larger body exercising legitimate claims on everyone in the situation" (McCall & Simmons, 1966 p. 159).

The predictions of exchange theory concerning the probability of an age-based social-political movement emerging in the *near* future are, without question, quite muddled. The muddle comes from the problematic applicability of the Rule of Distributive Justice. Homans argued that, according to the Rule of Distributive Justice, if the parties in an exchange interaction do not gain profits in proportion to their investments, they will feel anger. Truly, the aged in modern society are among those who rarely, if ever, enjoy a return in profits that is in proportion to their investments. Most old people have invested their entire lives in society through their work and the fulfillment of their family responsibilities, yet their rewards in terms of income, positions of prestige, autonomy, and status within the community fall far below the level of fair return on investment. Although the resource exchange rate is a function of the relative power of the exchange partners, the Rule of Distributive Justice presumably operates to prevent an *unfair* influence of power on the exchange rate. However, in their exchange relations with younger partners, old people do not appear to be obtaining profits in proportion to their investments; if this is the case; why haven't we seen the anger that Homans predicted?

One reason for the lack of anger on the part of old people may be their low level of age consciousness. In a recent study of age consciousness, for example, it was noted that the most age-conscious people in the United States are the unemployed, people who were forced to retire, homemakers, and the Black aged. However, the majority of the respondents—particularly the middle-class respondents—were not especially age conscious (Dowd, 1978b). (This is not to say that the aged never were or never will be age conscious. The Townsend Movement and the Gray Panther Movement[12] are evidence that an organized group of older citizens can emerge under certain economic and historical circumstances.)

One possible explanation for the lack of age consciousness on the part of old people may be that they estimate their investments to be lower and their profits or rewards to be higher than the estimates of researchers. This would

---

[12] The Townsend Movement originated in California during the 1930s for the purpose of supporting Dr. Francis Townsend's plan to provide a pension of $200 per month to those people over 65 who agreed to retire. The movement lost considerable momentum when, in 1935, the Social Security Act was passed. The Gray Panther Movement emerged in 1970 under the leadership of Margaret Kuhn; it includes both young and old members who believe that *ageism* can be fought more effectively by a group than by individuals.

be an example of the internalization of an ideology making an unfair distribution of rewards seem legitimate; that is, old people, by accepting society's dictum (ideology) that they are entitled to fewer social exchanges and less profit than other people, come to view their altered profit and investment levels as adequate. However, it is difficult to believe that old people could so grossly misperceive the levels of their investments and profits and so one still wonders where the anger is that Homans and others have predicted?

One possible solution to this dilemma is contained in the work on decision rules by Meeker (1971) and Cook (1977). For several years (at least since Homans' introduction of the Rule of Distributive Justice in 1961), exchange theory has spoken of social interaction as being governed by the justice rule. As rule-abiding people, we presumably act in the spirit of "fairness" when we negotiate a particular exchange rate. Yet the inherent conflict between justice and the natural drive to maximize profit has always constituted a weak stitch in the fabric of exchange theory. The development of the concept of **decision rule** constitutes an exciting development, because it suggests one possible way to correct the weakness. In essence, decision rules govern the negotiation of exchange rates. The adoption of a decision rule in any particular situation depends upon the interaction of elements in the situation. The Rule of Distributive Justice is only one decision rule; another is *rationality,* which is "an exchange rule that assigns to P the outcome that maximizes his total payoff" (Emerson, 1976, p. 353). Other rules that have been identified in laboratory studies as decision rules include altruism, competition, reciprocity, and status consistency. At this point, it is premature to try to predict which decision rule would apply in any one exchange situation. All we know is that several such rules exist and that they are "among the emergent attributes of exchange relations" (Emerson, 1976, p. 353).

The concept of decision rules has great significance for the study of social gerontology. One no longer needs to accept the premise that justice or even rationality underlies social exchange. Decision rules are definitions of the exchange situation that form among exchange partners and that specify what distribution is appropriate. Thus, the concepts of justice and equality may not apply to the case of cross-age interactions. Instead, the goal of status consistency may be the orientation that guides the interaction. This would explain the disinterest among some old people concerning what appears to be a failure of distributive justice.

Segregation of the Aged: A Prelude to Conflict?

In this chapter I have reviewed some recent developments in the conceptualization of exchange and have suggested ways in which these emerging concepts may increase our understanding of social behavior in old age. We have seen how *status generalization,* operating in conjunction with *the burden of proof principle,* has affected the bargaining position of old people in social exchange. Similarly, the concept of *decision rule* has been applied to account for the apparent failure of Homans' Rule of Distributive Justice to explain the lack of age consciousness among old people. This section will conclude the discussion of power, dependency, and old age by focusing on an important issue facing old people and gerontologists alike—age segregation—through the lens of exchange theory.

The issue of age-segregated living environments has been a topic of considerable discussion and research among social gerontologists, including exchange theorists, and it raises many questions. For example, is age-segregated housing a reasonable social policy? Is it ethically defensible? Wouldn't each generation suffer in its own way from the decrease in intergenerational contact? Will age segregation have political effects, such as an increased sense of political awareness among old people?

In general, age segregation erects **boundaries** among the different age groups. These boundaries are both physical and social in nature, and so they serve as an obstacle to interaction. From the exchange-theory perspective, intergenerational or cross-age contact is seen as a *boundary crossing* (Anderson & Davis, 1979). However, it would be a mistake to view age segregation as an onerous burden placed on old people by an uncaring society. Indeed, as discussed earlier, some age segregation is maintained by old people themselves as a strategy of minimizing the costs of social exchange. Also, interaction with age peers is the general rule for all age groups, and this suggests that such a pattern is rewarding for most people, including the aged. Collins, in his treatise on conflict sociology (1975), agrees that friendship formation among age peers is the product of choice, not constraint:

> Children of different ages, adolescents, unmarried young adults, the married middle-aged, and the elderly all tend to form distinct social circles . . . The main principle is clear: different age groups have interests and resources of their own, which they can maximally enjoy in their own company [p. 82].

Because they possess similar interests and share similar resources, the aged—like other age groups—tend to interact most frequently with their age peers. Since they often have fewer resources that would be perceived as rewarding to the middle-aged, old people tend not to have access to the opportunity structures promoting interaction among those in mid-life. In other words, when a person has few, if any, resources to exchange, it becomes less likely that the person will meet potential exchange partners (Suttles & Street, 1970). This "natural tendency" helps to explain why exchange relations tend to form among partners with similar power. Unbalanced exchanges—like, for example, the ones that characterize many cross-age interactions—are defined in terms of dependency and strength. Because dependency is undesirable in most cases, unbalanced exchanges tend to be avoided.

In this sense, age groups, like classes, may be conceived of as exchange *networks* in which *intra*category exchange has a much greater probability of occurrence than *inter*category exchange (Stolte & Emerson, 1977). In the language of structuralist theory (Blau, 1974), age is a nominal parameter that differentiates groups of people and "increases the preponderance of ingroup over intergroup associations" (Blau, 1977, p. 92). A comprehensive analysis of friendships and other social networks documents the low probability of cross-age friendships; the authors of the analysis describe the barriers as "extensive 'faults' in the age structure" (Fischer, Jackson, Stueve, Gerson, Jones, & Baldassare, 1977, p. 68). Even men who are close to either end of the "productive phase" of the life cycle[13]—that is, close to the ages of 21 and 65—are far more likely to choose their friends from within the 21–65 range than outside of it. Apparently, the existence of entry and exit points of labor-force participation reinforces the tendency toward age-graded friendship.

Consequently, even if the older person *chose* to remain engaged in the mainstream of social life through intergenerational contact, the age boundary would remain an obstacle. One reason for this, as mentioned previously, concerns the age similarity of friendship patterns. This suggests that, for less formal social interactions like those between friends or neighbors, individuals tend to select exchange partners similar to them in power. However, a second reason for age being an obstacle to intergenerational contact concerns the necessity of negotiating an age-relevant exchange rate and, more problematic, the ambiguity surrounding the appropriate *rule* for exchange. Thus, part of the boundary between any two age groups is created by the absence of routine expectations; that is, although rules are taken for granted in relations with age peers, they must be clarified and agreed upon in cross-generational relations. The process of establishing rules is described by Anderson and Davis (1979):

> one crucial aspect of cross-boundary social action must be *rule-work*. By this term we refer to activities by people in groups to clarify to themselves and others which norms or rules apply to the situation at hand and how, *concretely,* these norms are to be interpreted in that situation. For instance, before agreement can be reached about what constitutes fair or just exchange in a particular situation, the *relevant* social properties of the situation have to be agreed upon or at least formulated in ways acceptable to the parties: that is, the situation has to be *socially constructed* [pp. 5–6].

The enmity among generations that Lorenz and others believe to exist is much less of a factor in explaining the disinclination towards intergenerational exchange than is the mere necessity of *rule-work*. When older people are by themselves, such rule-work is unnecessary. Meanings are relatively uniform and, consequently, there is less need for precise language or, even, for language (in the form of conversation) at all. In most cases, a certain look, a wink, a nod or other gesture is all that is necessary. Hochschild's important

---

[13] This is Carlsson and Karlsson's (1970) phrase, not mine.

work, *The Unexpected Community* (1973), contains several illustrations of the emergence of common meanings in a community of old widows.

Crossing age boundaries is a journey that carries with it considerable costs. Because the power differential between age groups tends to favor the middle-aged, it is the middle-aged group that *assumes* "its discourse will dominate in its dealings" with the aged (Anderson & Davis, 1979). Consequently, prior to even entering into a negotiation of exchange rates, the old person must learn all of the relevant "taken-for-granteds" and shorthand phrases used by the middle-aged partner. Of course, as time passes, the power advantage may balance out and the aged person may choose to challenge the "hegemony" of the younger partner, but, even yet, considerable costs will have been incurred up to this point.

The title of this section is "Age Segregation: Prelude to Conflict?" Many role theorists who have written on this subject argue that it may indeed be so: age segregation may lead to age conflict through a channelization of interests (Baum & Baum, 1975; Foner, 1974; Riley, Johnson, & Foner, 1972, and Rose, 1965). Although the rationale underlying this argument is internally consistent, it ignores several facts about age-graded friendships. For example, age-graded friendships are more profitable for the old person and, consequently, produce satisfaction, not dissatisfaction, with existing arrangements. Furthermore, regardless of anyone's approval, such friendships are likely to predominate because they reflect the "faults" or boundaries inherent in our age-stratified society that preclude extensive age conflict.

Age conflict, should it emerge, will likely result from disagreement over exchange rates. This implies the existence of considerable cross-age contact, and, because of this, the probability of age conflict involving *old* people is fairly remote. The group most likely to become involved in renegotiation of exchange rates (because of re-evaluation of its "social worth")[14] is the group described by Neugarten (1974) as the "young-old" (those in the 55–75 age range). The group most likely to come into conflict with the "young-old" group may well be the stratum aged 35 to 55—those whose new knowledge places them among the higher echelons of modern technocracy. Because of the recognition and definition of the "young-old" age group, redefinition of entry points into other age strata is likely. For example, "old age" seems to be getting older, whereas middle age is getting younger all the time. Entry into "old age," based on functional or legal criteria, is now close to 70 and will probably reach 75 before the year 2000. In the process of defining entry and exit points for the later stages in the life cycle, exchange rates among the groups involved will also have to be redefined or renegotiated. I would argue that this renegotiation will be the factor that determines the presence or absence of age conflict. Should the "young-old" demand (through their actions and attitudes) to be perceived and evaluated as middle-

[14] For a discussion of social worth that is similar, in parts, to the exchange treatment of power, see Wittermans and Krauss (1964).

---

aged rather than old, the probability of conflict will increase. Such a demand would mean, in effect, that members of the group aged 35–55 would have to lower their customary profits—a change rarely accepted without conflict. Most of the initial discussions of the possible emergence of generational conflict involving the aged failed to take the shifting definition of entry points into age groups into account (see, for example, Binstock, 1972; Ragan & Dowd, 1974; Rose, 1965; and Ward, 1977).

Review Questions

1. *Describe what is meant by social structure.*
2. *From an exchange perspective, what are some ways in which older social actors can rebalance their relationships with younger social actors?*
3. *How are power and dependence related?*
4. *In what sense is every social act an exercise of power?*
5. *How are status characteristics involved in the process of negotiating exchange rates?*
6. *One cannot be powerful all by oneself. Why is this so?*
7. *In the conduct of social exchange, older people often find themselves in a "double bind." Explain.*
8. *What is meant by distributive justice?*
9. *Exchange relations have three general components: (1) psychological; (2) social psychological; and (3) sociological. Discuss.*
10. *Do exchange relations tend to become balanced over time? Discuss both the short-run and the long-run aspects of this question.*

4

The Power
of
Old People
and the
Modernization of
Society

There has been considerable research on age stratification in modern society that has examined changes in age status within a variety of historical contexts. In this chapter, I will review this literature and attempt to draw out its implications for an exchange theory of aging. More specifically, I will focus on two aspects of social change and relate each to the position of old people in modern society. The first aspect of social change, which will be examined in the present chapter, is change at the level of social structure. The discussion will include reference to the continuing debate within gerontology on the effects of **modernization** on age status, and it will attempt to extend this debate by directing consideration to two previously undeveloped aspects of modernization's effect on age status: 1) the influence of power resources on the legitimacy of social ranking; and 2) the effects of recent *structural* changes, on age status, particularly the transition of modern society in the United States from competitive capitalism to monopolistic capitalism. Chapter 5 will cover the second aspect of social change, *ideology,* and relate the ways in which structural and ideological evolution effect a gradual change in age status.

Sociology began when the French Revolution produced cataclysmic changes in the social relationships among groups in European society. In the context of industrialization, which was spreading across the European continent from England, the French Revolution was a watershed in social history. It was the event that caused social philosophers to debate the effects of change on society and that eventually led to the emergence of sociology as an academic discipline.

For sociological purposes, the French Revolution constituted one of a small number of historical events that defined a "before" and an "after". Sociologists began to use the French Revolution as the event, for example, that marked the passing of "traditional" society and the beginning of the modern era; it indexed the passing of the Ancien Régime and the advent of the age of bureaucracy. The concepts of the early sociologists reflected this dichotomous view of social history. Tönnies, for example, developed the classic Gemeinschaft-Gesellschaft distinction—the notion that modern society is based on the primacy of formalized rules, bureaucratic organization, and agreement by legal contracts, in contrast to the more personal and informal structure of previous periods.[1]

The distinction between traditional and modern societies has great relevance to the study of stratification and the aged. The bases of social status changed dramatically during industrialization from a system based on control of property (land) to one based on control of the means of economic production (factories and machines). The nature of the division of labor also changed with the Industrial Revolution from one based on ascription to one based more on achievement. Social status and one's social "worth" in modern society reflect the premium placed on efficiency, rationality, and productivity (Wittermans & Krauss, 1964).

Several writers have argued that the power of the aged in modern society has declined relative to the power they had in traditional societies. The reasons for this, it is argued, have to do with changes in social relationships caused by the introduction of new technology. In an industrial economy, knowledge becomes specialized. The development of modern communications and data storage systems effects a devaluation of both traditional knowl-

---

[1] Tönnies' work was only one of many typologies offered by sociologists to characterize the before/after phenomenon. Others include Becker's (1956) sacred and secular society; Durkheim's (1947) mechanical and organic solidarity; MacIver's (1927) communal and associational society; Maine's (1906) status and contract society; Redfield's (1947) folk and urban society; Sorokin's (1957) familistic and contractual society; and Zimmerman's (1938) localistic and cosmopolitan society. Several of these distinctions apply not only to situations of "before" and "after" but also to coexisting communities within the same society.

edge and the role of those who transmit the traditional culture. As argued by Bengtson, Dowd, Smith, and Inkeles (1975, p. 668), "knowledge and control gained by long experience no longer represent useful barter in economic and social exchange; under such conditions aging may lose whatever value it once represented."

One of the consequences of the shift from an agricultural to an industrialized economy (or, from a traditional to a modern social system) has been a decline in the power of old people relative to the power of other age groups (Burgess, 1960; Cowgill & Holmes, 1972; and Simmons, 1945). Empirical evidence generally supports the idea that old people lose status as modernization progresses. The status of the aged (as measured by relative income, health, weeks worked, and education) was higher in the United States, for example, in 1940 than in 1969 (Palmore & Whittington, 1971). A study by Palmore and Manton also reported that, in comparison to younger age groups, the status of old people is lower in modern societies (those with a high GNP and a greater proportion of workers in industry than in agriculture) than in societies described as "traditional" or "developing" (1974). Basing their work on such observations, Cowgill and Holmes (1972) developed a generalized theory of aging. These authors attempt to demonstrate that the decline in prestige that comes with aging in modern societies is due primarily to urbanization, the development of new technology, and the elimination of illiteracy. Each of these factors serves to increase the status and functional importance of youth in modern society. Educational systems, for example, generally focus on the younger age groups in industrialized societies—a development that negates the traditional value of the "wise" elder who possessed the sacred knowledge of the group's past.

Although the modernization hypothesis continues to find wide application in social gerontology, several writers have questioned the validity of the theory, particularly the implication that the aged were relatively better off in traditional societies. Some criticize this notion as "naive" or "romanticized" (Harlan, 1964; Slater, 1964); for example, Lipman (1970) suggests that researchers may have misinterpreted the "ritual deference" accorded old people in traditional societies as indicative of their high status. A more realistic approach, according to Lipman, would show that the actual status of the aged in traditional societies was low.

A similar conclusion is drawn by other researchers who question the deleterious impact of modernization on *relative* age status. Although they do not make a strict comparison of pre- and post-industrialized societies, some of these critics point to cross-cultural evidence that suggests no great differences in age status. Neugarten and Hagestad (1976) claim, for example, that "presently available studies of older persons in other societies raise doubts about the stereotyped view that the aged have lost status as a consequence of urbanization and industrialization" (p. 38). Other critics, such as Inkeles, see nothing about modern life that, in itself, has a corrosive impact upon the prestige of old people:

Nothing in urban living *per se* requires a person to show disrespect for the aged, and nothing in industrial experience explicitly teaches a man to abandon the aged. Many an old man and woman in the villages have been abandoned by their children because the children lacked the means to support them. Steadier wages and generally more stable conditions of life for those gainfully employed in industry could well enable those who enjoyed these benefits to be more exacting in their fulfillment of obligations to old people. And they might well be as respectful of the aged as their more traditional counterparts farming in the villages [1973, p. 164].

The major critic of the modernization theory has been the historical sociologist Laslett (1976). Laslett argues that the modernization hypothesis is another manifestation of the "world we have lost" syndrome—the tendency to view the deficiencies of the present as resulting from "the destruction of an idealized society at some point in the past" (p. 91). Laslett's major target is the belief in the era of the extended family—the belief in the existence of a past time when the aged were integrated into three-generational families and held important roles within them. Laslett believes this precept to be a myth, and, therefore, he argues that the modernization thesis is flawed. However, it should be noted that a hypothesis of an extended-family era never played a central role in the modernization theory of age status, as developed by Cowgill (Cowgill & Holmes, 1972; Cowgill, 1974a, 1974b). Indeed, Laslett never even mentions the contributions of Cowgill or Palmore to the modernization thesis. The precise identity of the proponents of the extended-family myth are never revealed by Laslett, although it seems apparent that they are members of the tribe of family sociology rather than social gerontology.

The confusion in Laslett's argument against the modernization theory seems to derive from his desire to demonstrate that previous generations were not morally superior to current generations. Indeed, Laslett never directly addresses the central issue of the aged's status loss in modern societies; instead, he is concerned with proving the absence of any statutes reflecting the aged's alleged higher status in pre-industrial societies. Presumably, if there were no laws favoring old people, their status could not have been very high. However, even if the existence of such legislation could be proved, the issue of changes in age status could never be explained on the basis of legal regulations or any other formal code. The major medium of status conferral, as we discussed in the last chapter, is informal deference rituals. Laslett confuses the issue by asserting the primacy of legal sanctions over informal norms and rules. The relationship between legal sanctions and informal rules and norms is highly variable and, in most cases, knowledge of the former does not imply knowledge of the latter. Because of this and other inconsistencies, Laslett can only conclude that the prestige and respect accorded the old in modern societies is fairly high and that, even if our current treatment of the aged is occasionally reprehensible, one cannot hope to restore structural relationships of past eras. Laslett believes that our ancestors probably behaved toward their elders much as we do now (1976, p. 96): "the most likely conjecture . . . is that they behaved very much as we behave now in this respect, no better and no worse."

Although there have been many other studies on the topic of modernization's effect on age status, they also do not all agree. Some suggest, quite correctly, that physical survival in today's society is much less problematic for old people than it was earlier (Slater, 1964). Others observe, again correctly, that the *relative* position of the aged has declined with modernization. However, although each of these positions is well supported and cannot be ignored at this point, one thing remains missing from all of them: a framework for analysis that would incorporate the nagging exceptions, such as the examples of low status of the aged in pre-industrial settings or high status of old people in modern societies.

From the vantage point of exchange theory, any analysis of power and deference relations must be grounded in an analysis of the *relative* resources of the groups involved. A significant proviso of an exchange analysis of the modernization thesis is that the analysis must consider the exceptional case. In general, exchange analysis shows that, as the economic distributive systems of societies increase in complexity, the relative power of the aged, vis-à-vis younger groups, declines. In exchange terms, this suggests only that, on the *average,* the proportion of society's surplus possessed by the aged declines with the progress of modernization.

However, such a description need not blind us to the existence of cases that are outside the average range. In every historical period, there have been generational "units" that were able to attain greater-than-average power and status because they possessed a disproportionately large share of the available resources.

One's access to several of the categories of power resources is a function of status, or social ranking. As the relative ranking of a group within the existing social structure changes, the relative power of members of that group changes correspondingly. The recent change in the social status of women and Blacks, for example, has increased their power as well. This is not to suggest that the resources of all Blacks or all women have increased; rather, it is the average power of these groups at two different points in time that is being compared.

In any case, regardless of the amount and quality of one's resources, historical factors must be considered, because the significance of one level of access to resources, and the privilege that comes with it, varies according to socio-historical context. Consequently, in monopolistic-capitalistic societies, the aged are required to expend a greater amount of resources than old people in traditional societies in order to accrue the same proportion of privilege.[2]

[2]I exclude from the term *traditional societies* those societies described by political economists as both authoritarian (rather than polyarchic) and without "market-oriented" economic systems. Such societies include most of the Communist systems (except Yugoslavia and, perhaps, Hungary) as well as Nazi Germany (cf., Lindblom, 1977). Because of the inaccessibility of data for these societies, describing the relative power of their aged populations would be difficult.

Although it is still possible for old people to obtain high status in modern societies, the unfavorable exchange rates makes this less likely than in previous eras. In modern society, the old person with a relatively large share of valuable resources is handicapped in negotiations of exchange rates because of the possession of a devalued status characteristic—old age. Blau (1977, p. 151) explains this problem succinctly: "pronounced differences in social resources between groups give rise to social processes that transform great average differences in resources (status) between groups into categorical status differences rooted in group membership as such, independent of an individual's own resources."

In summary, it is generally true that the greater the amount of resources available to a social actor, the greater the proportion of privilege he or she can expect to obtain. At the same time, however, this relationship is affected by the prevailing exchange rates, and the exchange rates may favor different exchange partners at different times.

The major determinant of exchange rates in any historical era is the distribution of power resources. The power of social actors is a function of their relative share of privilege (and not necessarily of their relationship to the means of production). In early **hunting and gathering societies,** a major determinant of power was natural ability, particularly *strength*. In such societies, as described by de Beauvoir (1972), the position of the aged was wretched. She notes that "where the climate is severe, the environment harsh and the resources inadequate, human old age often resembles that of the animals" (p. 45).[3] She cites the case of the Siberian Yakuts, among whom the father ruled in tyrannical fashion, but only as long as he retained his strength; when his strength ebbed because of age or illness, de Beauvoir notes that "his sons took his possessions from him by force and let him more or less perish" (1972, p. 45). Similar examples of this pattern are found among the Siriono of Bolivia, the Fang of the Gabon Republic, the Thonga of South Africa, and others; in each case, the aged have little prestige and few resources. Even the possession and transmission of knowledge could not be used as a resource by the aged in these groups, because these groups have no heritage of cultural or social tradition or religious rituals to remember and pass on. Additional information on the aged in undeveloped societies has been provided by Sheehan, who analyzed the large mass of data available in HRAF (Human Resources Area Files); he concluded that "seniors in nomadic or semipermanent societies are held in low regard compared to their counterparts in more developed societies. There exist few material resources for them to accumulate or over which to build control" (1976, p. 435).

In contrast to the type of societies just cited, according to de Beauvoir, societies that value magic or religious rituals usually accord the aged a high

---

[3] This and all other quotations from this source are reprinted by permission of G. P. Putnam's Sons from *The Coming of Age,* by Simone de Beauvoir. English translation copyright © 1972 by Andre Deutsch, Weidenfeld and Nicolson, and by G. P. Putnam's Sons.

position in the group. As examples of such groups, de Beauvoir lists, among others, the Navajo, the Tiv of Nigeria, and the Zande of the Sudan. However, although de Beauvoir presents an informative historical overview, she errs at several points in her statement on the general status of old people. Because, in most societies, old people are not "producers," de Beauvoir incorrectly concludes that their status is merely a "granted" one. She fails to realize that control over rituals or political tradition is as much a resource in many societies as control over land or factories. She presumes, again incorrectly, that the aged *never* have any real power, and that their status always depends on whether their resources—whatever they may be—serve the interests of the group that always posseses the real power—that is, the middle-aged. Contrary to de Beauvoir's view, however, when old people enjoy high status in a society, it is because their resources are in fact powerful in relation to the resources of other people, and not because their status is "granted" to them. Indeed, it is a gross distortion to suggest, as de Beauvoir (1972, p. 89) does, that the status of the aged is "never subject to any sort of development," and that "it is the middle-aged who decide, according to their own interests, practical and ideological, the role that can most suitably be given to the aged."

Yet, even with the rhetorical excesses that abound in the *Coming of Age,* the work of de Beauvoir contributes greatly to our understanding of the relationship between age status and social structure. It is because of this work that it has become possible to extend the modernization thesis to previous historical periods. Through de Beauvoir's analysis of the Dark Ages, for example, it becomes clear that the historical evolution of the status of old people resembles a curvilinear (inverted U-shaped) trend, rather than a negative linear one. The status of the aged seems to have increased considerably between the 13th and 18th centuries. The major occurrence that enhanced the position of old people around the 13th century was the development of a system of legal contracts governing the ownership of land. Previously, one "owned" land only if one could defend it—a system clearly disadvantageous to the old. Under the new system, ownership of land was based upon legally recognized titles, and this system altered the status of the aged who were able to buy land. The 18th century saw the status of old people, particularly those in middle-class society, reach its zenith. In old age, de Beauvoir notes, "the head of the family remained in control of his property and he enjoyed his economic standing. The respect that he inspired took on a sentimental form . . . " (1972, p. 183).

The status of the aged in the New World was apparently also quite high during the period prior to industrialization. The excellent study of aging in America by the historian Fischer (1977), for example, described the period from 1607 to 1780 as the "Exaltation of Age in Early America." Some historians, however, disagree with Fischer's assessment, pointing, as Smith (1978) does, to the withering during the 18th century of "the older matrix of values sustaining respect for the aged" (p. 296). However, from a sociological view, power and social position are not necessarily described by a society's social values. The fact that, during this century, a set of values that encouraged respect for old people eroded, may actually support, rather than disconfirm, the idea that the power and prestige of the aged were at their apogee in the 18th century. Values are important sources of protection for the weak and dispossessed. The powerful, because of their disproportionate share of a finite set of resources, are often a target of hostility rather than an object of sympathy. During the early part of the 18th century, old people seem to have been feared and respected, if not loved.

By most accounts, the "great transformation" in the status of the aged occurred with industrialization, because legal land ownership in an industrial economy brought the landowner less status than in the previous agricultural economy. Factory work increasingly became the major occupational pursuit, creating the two large social classes of capitalists and workers. The position of most old people in 19th-century Europe closely resembled that of the proletariat. In general, the changes that accompanied industrialization were, as de Beauvoir notes, "disastrous for the old" (1972, p. 193):

> Neither in France nor in England had their condition been so cruelly hard as it was in the second half of the nineteenth century. Labor was not protected . . . As they grew old, the workers were unable to keep up with the rhythm . . . In every country, those who managed to survive were reduced to extreme poverty when their age deprived them of their jobs.

The reader should note that this discussion focuses on the aged in industrialized, Western societies. Clearly, the 19th century was not experienced similarly by old people in other societies. Indeed, in non-industrialized societies, the dominance of the aged continued. Accounts of scientists and missionaries who visited parts of the non-industrialized world during this period confirm that the political, social, and economic aspects of life in these societies were firmly under the control of old people, including old women (Landtman, 1938). (This does not mean, however, that *all* old people in these societies retained considerable power; there are always exceptions to the rule.) As in all other societies at any time, the respect and consideration shown to old people in non-industrialized societies lessened as the physical and mental abilities of the aged declined. Older people in modern societies who remain engaged in positions of considerable authority—political leaders, for example—are particularly vulnerable and sensitive to the loss of power associated with physical decline.[4]

The necessity of a social-class analysis of the status of the aged becomes clear in light of the profound changes in social relationships that accompanied the Industrial Revolution. In addition to changing the way goods are produced, the Industrial Revolution produced fundamental value changes

---

[4] For an interesting account of the ways political leaders attempt to disguise their health problems in an effort to forestall any loss of power, see Halberstam's (1979) analysis, in which he discusses Sam Rayburn and Franklin D. Roosevelt.

that became evident in the politics, law, ideology, arts, and science of the late 18th/early 19th century. It was this great social revolution, according to Fischer (1977), that "created a world without 'veneration' on the one hand or 'condescension' on the other; a world without eldership or primogeniture." Society was becoming youth oriented. The differences between the styles of life led by old people in the various social classes grew even larger during this period, and they became so great by the late 19th century as to lead some to suggest that "one might almost be looking at different species" (de Beauvoir, 1972, p. 198).

The upper classes grew wealthy by lending money; within these classes, aging was associated with an accumulation of wealth. For the workers, however, old age was a period of desperate poverty. Even with the growth of the labor movement, the position of the aged was not perceptibly changed. During much of the initial phase of the labor movement, the focus of concern was the younger worker, not the retiree. In an excellent study of the history of pensions in France, Stearns (1976) notes that serious concern over the plight of the older worker could be discerned only around 1971: "until this point it seemed that neither variations nor evolutions of ideology produced any real division over the importance of older workers, who were to be commiserated with but largely ignored" (1976, p. 62).

So, for people in industrialized societies in the 19th century, the concept of old age was almost foreign. Life was characterized by a period of work that ended when the worker became incapacitated and that was quickly followed by the worker's death. Among the working class during the late 19th century, there was no concept of a distinct period of life called old age.

Old Age in the 20th Century

The 20th century presents its own distinct challenge to analysts seeking a definitive resolution to the question of the status of the aged. Although the *absolute* condition of old people has undoubtedly improved since the end of the 19th century, research has demonstrated that their *relative* position has not improved. Some researchers, in fact, argue that the relative power of the aged has declined in the 20th century because experience has been discredited as a power resource. Modern technocratic society, in the words of de Beauvoir (1972, p. 210), "thinks that knowledge does not accumulate with the years, but grows out of date."

In any case, whether or not the status of old people in a modern industrialized society has changed in comparison to the status of the aged in other societies, the sheer numbers of old people alive today make their exclusion from policy considerations highly improbable. Their numbers have grown over the past century and, with the increase, old-age social policies have begun to evolve. The extent of the coverage and benefits of the various social security systems in Western societies, for example, is largely a function of the sheer numbers of old people in these societies (Wilensky, 1975).

As is characteristic of all stratification systems, however, an increase in size of a class brings with it an increase in *social distance* (Abrahamson, Mizruchi, & Hornung, 1976). One manifestation of social distance in age-stratification systems has been the devaluation of the aged. Whereas in agrarian mid-19th century America, as Achenbaum (1974) notes, the aged were revered as the fittest, since they survived the longest, the sharp increase in the numbers of those surviving into old age in the 20th century negated this particular source of prestige. Thus, although the material condition of old people in our time has improved markedly, a new set of factors has emerged that has worked to old people's disadvantage in a new way. Modern writers have described the 20th century as a period of depersonalization or deinstitutionalization. The ties that bound together the citizens of earlier periods gradually weakened or disappeared with the progress of industrialization in modern society. With the coming of "post-industrial" society (cf. Bell, 1973), stratification systems became more structured,[5] making the exchange rates that exist at the group level less susceptible to modification by individuals. According to some stratification theorists, "these impersonal processes reinforce *structured* social inequalities by treating persons as objects rather than subjects" (Abrahamson et al., 1976, p. 12).

When discussing the problems and status of the aged in the 20th century, one realizes that the main factor that determines the nature of intergenerational relations in Western societies is the society's political economy. In other 20th century societies where the relative power of the aged remains fairly high, industrialization has yet to be introduced on a large scale.[6] For example, in modern socialist China, the aged maintain a fairly constant level of resources and, hence, a relatively larger degree of power than their counterparts in the West (Ganschow, 1978; Treas, 1978). According to Treas,

---

[5]The question of the continued relevance of social-class analyses for contemporary society has been raised by some theorists, who argue that the greater availability of material resources to all citizens, regardless of class background, has led to a merging of the working class with the larger middle class. This presumed "embourgeoisement" of society has formed the basis of many recent political works, including studies of public opinion (Wattenberg, 1976). Some political writers have argued that generational differences have become more important today because of the embourgeoisement of the worker. Abramson (1975), for example, has recently argued that "economic prosperity tends to reduce class divisions. In a prosperous society, the different material rewards that the working and middle classes receive are increasingly narrowed. . . . In an advanced industrial economy the middle class . . . tends to expand." From a sociological perspective, however, the embourgeoisiement thesis is not supported by the empirical data. Using categories of class identification argued by neo-Marxist writers such as Anderson (1974), Wright (1976), and Wright and Perrone (1977), the continued validity of a class analysis is suggested. In fact, some writers suggest that the "proletarianization" of segments of the middle class is a more apt description of current reality (cf. Carchedi, 1977; Horowitz, 1977; Levison, 1975; Lockwood, 1960; and Porter, 1965).

[6]Available evidence indicates that Japan may be an exception to the rule that industrialization lowers the prestige of old people.

in family life as well, the old seem to maintain their high status, generally commanding the respect and support of younger generations. In the country-side, this reflects not only a persistence of traditional values, but also a continuation of the economic interdependence of generations . . . Parents continue to control the family purse strings and inheritable assets. Parents continue to provide valuable services such as child care and gardening. In cities, too, the old enjoy a secure place in family life. They, too, furnish valuable services, and nowadays they also contribute a pension which com-pares favorably with worker wages [1978, p. 12].

In societies, however, where industrialization is advanced, problems arise that are specific to their type of political economy. For example, Kreps, prior to assuming her position as Secretary of Commerce in the Carter ad-ministration, noted that one of the inherent contradictions in the American capitalistic economy is the position of retirees: "the faster the pace of the economy's growth and the longer the retirement period, the greater the dete-rioration in relative income position of retirees" (1976, p. 274). Other research-ers note that, although retirement may not be a particular boon to the economic position of old people in American society, neither is continued employment. Declines in health and strength produce greater negative effects on earnings than the accumulation of seniority and experience can compen-sate for. Because of this, the relationship between age and earnings is nega-tive for older workers (Stolzenberg, 1975b). In other words, the increments to income usually obtained through seniority cease for the older worker. For workers past the age of 50, earnings may even decrease because of the increasing number of health disability days that are associated with the in-creased age of the worker.

The "Dual Economy" and Old People

Hidden among all of the statistics and accounts of the problems faced by old people in modern American society is the simple fact that some old people live fairly well while others face certain impoverishment. This fact has nothing to do with individual skills, abilities, personality attributes, or other personal qualities; rather, it has to do with social structure. By *social struc-ture,* I mean the division of the American economy into sectors: one sector is highly organized and characterized by high wages and pension systems, and the other is marked by low wages and few, if any, fringe benefits.

The "dual-economy" theory on labor markets, which was discussed briefly in Chapter 1, has important implications for a study of older workers. The dual-economy theory emphasizes the income differences among groups of workers whose jobs are located in different economic sectors; that is, rather than emphasizing the relationship between a worker's income and personal characteristics, this theory directs our attention to the income levels that characterize different economic sectors. The dual-economy theory is opposite to the "human capital" theory (Becker, 1964), or the orthodox labor-market theory of neo-classical economists. The latter theories take the view that employers—because they are rational and want to maximize profits—tend to evaluate workers principally in terms of their individual characteristics, such as education or level of training. From this perspective, any labor-market differences among groups of workers—for example, between Black and White workers—"will decline over time because of competitive mechanisms" (Reich, Gordon, & Edwards, 1977, p. 108). However, the absence of an explanation for the continuing disparities in occupational placement and income among groups of workers remains a glaring omission in neo-classical theory.

In order to account for the disparities that neo-classical theory did not explain, sociologists and economists developed the "labor market segmentation" aspect of "dual-economy" theory. Although all sociologists and economists do not agree on all points of this theory, most of them agree on one important point: the American economic system has evolved since the latter part of the 19th century from a system of relatively small and numerous firms (competitive capitalism) to a system dominated by a few large corporations (monopolistic capitalism). In 1909, for example, only 15.3% of all employees in the United States worked in firms of over 1000 people. By 1955, however, this proportion had grown to 33.6% (Mandel, 1971). By 1962, the five largest corporations in the United States held over 12% of all manufacturing assets (Giddens, 1973). In addition, monopolistic—or late—capitalism differs from the early phase of competitive capitalism in that it designates a stage of capitalism "where, even given a number of large corporations operating within the same market, a monopoly operates, in so far as prices are fixed (jointly, by the corporations) and price-war is seriously curbed . . . and prices show a manipulated, steadily upward trend" (Slater, 1977, p. 16).

The transition to monopolistic capitalism[7] has not affected all industries equally; the trend toward monopolistic capitalism is much less evident in agriculture, nondurable manufacturing, and retail trade than it is in durable manufacturing, the construction trades, and the extraction industries (Bluestone, Murphy, & Stevenson, 1973). The fact that this transition occurred in some industries, but not in others, has created and perpetuated "segmented" labor markets. Ironically, it is those industries that remain closer to the "laissez-faire" ideal of competitive capitalism that provide the lowest wages and fewest fringe benefits. This is because oligopoly heightens profits within the "core" economic sector, which serves to intensify competition within "periphery" industries and, as a consequence, reduces profits within the periphery. As a result, competitive-sector workers suffer: "on the other hand,

---

[7]For an extended discussion of the characteristics of monopolistic capitalism, see Poulantzas (1975), Baran and Sweezy (1966), or Slater, (1977).

their wages are relatively low; on the other, they have to buy at relatively high monopolistic prices" (O'Connor, 1973, p. 22).

The firms in monopolistic-capitalistic industries are, on the average, large and unionized, and they generally make high profits and pay high wages. They are also characterized by a labor force disproportionately populated by White males. Although Black workers are to be found in certain core industries, such as automobile manufacturing, they make up the greatest proportion of workers in the peripheral industries (Bonacich, 1975; 1976). These peripheral industries generally are non-union, and they make lower profits and employ larger numbers of women and minority workers than core industries. Workers employed in peripheral industries have been described by Miller (1965) as the "new" working class.

The American economy is, in effect, a dual economy with a segmented labor market. Workers in "secondary" labor markets (markets that supply labor to peripheral industries) earn less than workers with comparable skills and training in "primary" labor markets. Older males who return to the labor force after retirement and older women are confined to this secondary labor market, along with ethnic minorities and children (Ng, 1977).

The relationship between unionization (a major factor differentiating primary and secondary labor markets) and age-earnings profile[8] has been studied by Stolzenberg (1975b). His analysis supports the hypothesis that the age-earnings profiles—that is, the graphic depiction of average earnings by age—of workers in unionized occupations "decline *less* after they peak than the age-earnings profiles of incumbents of less heavily unionized occupations" (1975b, p. 661). Stolzenberg shows, in a very careful analysis, how the age-earnings profiles for bus and truck drivers (who have a unionization rate of about 40%) fall more sharply after they reach their peak than the profiles of locomotive engineers and locomotive firemen (who are among the most heavily unionized workers in an industry that has about 79% of all of its employees in unions).

The differences between economic sectors do not end with income but include differences between pension plans and health insurance benefits; thus, a worker's life is affected by sector placement, even after retirement. Although an analysis has yet to be done, there is sufficient evidence to lead one to hypothesize that income differences among retired old people are a direct result of their sectoral location as workers. Contrary to the simplistic theories that the problems of the aged are caused by inadequate budget planning or poor household management, such a hypothesis suggests that the focus of explanations of aging "careers" should be at the structural—and not the individual—level. Differences between social classes continue to exist in old age. Indeed, one of the main effects of social class is to produce two distinct styles of aging.

---

[8] Age-earnings profiles are invariably curvilinear (inverted U-shaped), with the peak earnings occurring generally in middle age.

1. *Explain why industrialization has produced shifts in the status of old people.*
2. *Research in stratification recently has identified two major sectors in our economy. What are these sectors? How is the "dual economy" theory relevant to a study of aging?*
3. *Why are knowledge and experience less useful to the old person in modern society than to the old person in traditional society?*
4. *As societies undergo industrialization, do both the absolute and relative status of old people change? If so, how?*
5. *During what historical period did the relative position of the aged reach its height? Why?*
6. *Does the number of old people in a society affect the nature of old age social policy in that society? If yes, why and in what ways?*

5

The Aged in a Modern World: Alienation and Class Consciousness

As we have seen, the social bargaining position of old people is directly related to the amount of resources they possess and indirectly related to the nature of the existing social structures. Several of these indirect "structural" effects have already been discussed. Social structure affects, for example, the amount of a person's resources because it governs the distribution of society's surplus (privilege). I have also discussed the ways *status characteristics,* such as age, race, or sex, operate to affect *exchange rates* through the positive or negative connotation attached to each status characteristic. In the last chapter, the concept of dual economy, or "split-labor market," was introduced to show how the resources of some people are further limited, because these people are channeled into secondary labor markets.

All of these structural (or extra-individual) variables affect the individual at every phase of life. Even in retirement, when a worker ceases active competition in labor markets, the limitations and distinctions that attached to the worker's prior "structural position" will persist. The reasons for this persistence are only partially economic; that is, income level differences and changes are only part of the explanation. The bargaining position of old people in modern societies is also influenced by prevailing *ideologies*.

At least since Marx, sociologists have been sensitive to the ways groups that possess a disproportionately large share of resources attempt to legitimate their power through ideological arguments. One such argument is Darwin's "survival-of-the-fittest" idea, which nicely supported the actions and the interests of America's "robber barons" of the late 19th century. Another such ideology is the notion of America as a "classless" society, which people in power may quote to defuse other people's resentment of them as The Upper Class. In the case of the aged, America's support of "disengagement" in the form of forced retirement and generational succession within families may also be viewed as an ideology that serves the interests of one group over those of another.

In this chapter, I will continue the discussion of society's modernization, but I will switch the focus from changes in social and economic structures to the evolution of dominant ideologies that affect the aged. Of course, dominant ideologies and economics are always related to each other, and so, at some point, the two must be discussed jointly. This chapter will trace the emergence of the current ideology of modernity to its roots in the 19th-century movement toward bureaucratization and it will relate this ideology to the increased alienation of old people today, which is consistently evidenced in empirical studies and which is not a case of **normlessness** or **role strain** but, rather, evidence of an incipient **class consciousness** among old people.

The Nature of Dominant Ideologies

A natural inclination among exchange- and conflict-theory sociologists, when they are confronted with any social arrangement, is to ask the question "who benefits?"[1] This question means that value systems must be investigated in order to understand any social arrangement. In essence, the conflict and exchange perspectives have similar understandings of the emergence and persistence of values and beliefs; namely, they exist in order to enhance the structural position of a particular group or groups within the society.

Groups in control of economic and political institutions tend to perpetuate the values and beliefs that will preserve the status quo; subordinate groups, on the other hand, develop opposing ideologies that support the establishment of a new, revolutionary social order; and big business argues against government intervention while the poor plead for greater government assistance.

---

[1] For example, who benefits from the existence of segmented labor markets? According to Piore (1977), it is employers who benefit, because they are supplied through these markets with a low-cost supply of labor.

Each group, however, in order to gain support and a wider audience, must couch its principles in terms of general interest—not strictly in terms of its own narrow self-interests. Thus corporations issue statements (and make contributions) in support of the "free-enterprise system" or "individual freedom." Advocates for the poor speak of the "universal brotherhood of man," the "waste of human resources," the "responsibility of concerned citizens," the government as the "voice of the average citizen," and so on.

Mannheim termed the views of opposing groups *ideologies* and *utopias*. It is generally true that the ideology supporting the interests of the dominant class becomes the *dominant ideology*—a "set of beliefs that dominates all others and that, through its incorporation in the consciousness of subordinate classes, tends to inhibit the development of radical political dissent" (Abercrombie & Turner, 1978, p. 149). The dominant ideology, in many cases, is accepted not only by the dominant class, but also by the subordinate classes. For example, most working-class people in American society accept—and would fight to defend—the free-enterprise system, even though their interests would likely be better served by greater government intervention in the economic sphere.[2] From the position of the dominant class, this common adherence to a "central value system" is desirable because of the resultant stability and social order, and because it can be used as a means to suppress any change in the existent structure.

Any discussion of a dominant ideology requires the identification of the group that benefits from the ideology's existence; in other words, one must discuss the existence of dominant and subordinate classes. The existence of these classes, however, is by no means a decided issue. De Tocqueville, for example, argued that social class declined in importance as a parameter of social structure during the 19th century. Furthermore, he posited that the "ruling class"—meaning those whose wealth was derived from industrial production—possessed neither a class consciousness nor an ideology (in Nisbet, 1966). In similar fashion, Shils (1975) infers from the decline of aristocracy that the cohesiveness of ruling classes has diminished.

Other authors believe that both ruling classes *and* dominant ideologies remain intact in 20th-century societies, although in different form. Furthermore, they believe that the emergence of individualism in the 19th century, which led Tocqueville and others to conclude that the ruling class was coming apart, merely signified the ascendance of the ideology of the *new* ruling class—the capitalist class.

The new ruling class in industrialized society, the capitalist class, has been defined as those "who own and/or manage business firms, or who have primary kinship ties to those holding such positions" (Useem, 1978, p. 225). In America, this upper class probably emerged only towards the end of the 19th century, coinciding with the country's transition from competitive to monopolistic capitalism. Most of the members of this new upper class origi-

[2] See Veblen's analysis of *The Vested Interests and the Common Man* (1919).

nally lived in the Northeast and, even today, this class is primarily centered in the East (Giddens, 1973). In the United States, as contrasted with Europe, today's upper class is essentially a "business aristocracy." The real influence within this capitalist class is held by a small "inner group," whose members "exercise simultaneous influence over the activities of at least several major business firms" (Useem, 1978, p. 226). The existence of such an inner group is supported by a growing number of studies that document an extensive network of interlocking ties among major industrial and financial organizations.[3]

Although some may disagree with the proposition that an inner group of the capitalist class forms a "ruling" class, it would be difficult not to agree that owners and managers of corporations all share similar views of the role of business in society. (A content analysis of public speeches of corporate executives does, for example, reveal the presence of what may be called a *big business ideology* (Seider, 1974.) In general, however, the evidence does tend to support the existence of a dominant American class, which comprises the inner group of the capitalist class, which, in turn, is characterized by a particular view of the role of business in society. Can we conclude from this that a dominant ideology exists in America that serves to suppress revolutionary political activity among the subordinate classes? I would say "no," although I do believe that American society is *influenced* by a certain belief system that operates against the interests of subordinate classes, including the aged. This belief system, which I would term *modernity,* is an outgrowth of the transition from early, or competitive, capitalism to late, or monopolistic, capitalism.

During the transition from early to late capitalism, the control over business firms left the hands of the family and went to the corporation. Initially, families controlled the firms and were responsible for raising operating capital; at this time, government intervention in business was less than it is today. Although these firms did not have to tolerate much government intervention, however, they thereby lacked legal, or official, legitimation. According to Abercrombie and Turner, the economic functioning of a family-owned firm during the period of competitive capitalism required that the capitalist class develop and sustain a belief syetem, or ideology, that would legitimate their privileged position. After the transition to late capitalism, when capital was now raised through financial institutions, such as banks, pension funds, stock markets, and the state, and where government intervention is a factor, neither a cohesive "ruling class" nor a "dominant ideology" is necessary to protect the interests of the capitalist class. Legitimation adheres, in modern times, to official procedures, laws, and regulations. Government and business —or what Lindblom (1977) terms *politics* and *markets* —have become inevitably joined to support each other's interests.

---

[3] For additional information on "interlocking directorates," the reader is directed to the following material: Allen (1974); Domhoff (1974, 1975); Dooley (1969); Freitag (1975); Mariolis (1975); Miller (1978); Sonquist and Koenig (1975); Soref (1976); and Zeitlin (1974).

During the transition from early to late capitalism, the size of the state also increased dramatically. The threat of bureaucracy that concerned Weber in the 19th century continues to exist, with even more pernicious consequences, in the 20th century. One such consequence, as noted by Bell (1973), is the rise of a new force in modern society—a group that administers the bureaucracy of government and thereby influences the lives of individual citizens. In Bell's opinion, this group constitutes a new power in post-industrial society; he calls its members *technocrats*—that is, highly educated civil servants who possess the specialized knowledge necessary to formulate government policies.

The rise of technocracy in America has changed the relationship between the government and its citizens. As I will attempt to demonstrate in the next section, the subordinate classes—including the aged—have become estranged from dominant societal institutions, particularly since the post-World War II economic expansion. Modernization has undermined both the economic base of the aged as a class and the ideological or value basis for the deference that used to be granted to old people. Traditional values of integrity, loyalty, fairness, and "godfearingness" constituted, at one time, a resource that could be used by the aged—and other relatively powerless groups—in their negotiation of exchange rates. However, the transition to the new ideology of modernity, in which efficiency, productivity, and cost-effectiveness are the guiding values, has effectively diminished the average status of old people.

The "Iron Cage" of Bureaucracy

Apprehension about the growth of bureaucracy is not a recent phenomenon, it has been a continuing concern among sociologists for over 100 years. In 19th-century Germany, for example, the transition from Prussian Junkerdom to an industrialized state under Bismarck was the impetus for Tönnies' classic work, *Gemeinschaft und Gesellschaft*. The inspiration for Tönnies' masterpiece was his belief in "an antiprogressist view of society, one that saw the better forms of human interaction locked permanently in the past" (Mitzman, 1973, p. 23).

Another German sociologist who was concerned about the rise in bureaucracy is Max Weber. Weber, like Marx, saw great dangers in the growing rationalization of modern society. His fear was that society was becoming rationalized and administered "to the point where human beings emerge as virtual prisoners in an 'iron cage' of bureaucratic controls" (Greisman & Ritzer, 1978). Weber saw the future as a dehumanized time of total bureaucracy, with no room for individual autonomy. Indeed, both Weber and Marx understood the relationship between dehumanization and the transition to a capitalist political economy. The problem with a rationalized, free-enterprise system, in Weber's view, was its subversion of the traditional values. He argued, for example, that the "free markets" of capitalism lacked normative constraints, exploited the poor, tended toward monopolistic control, and, for all these reasons, was "an abomination to every system of fraternal ethics" (Weber, 1968, p.637).

Marx and Weber, however, did not agree on what the key issue would be for future generations struggling to survive. Marx believed that the key issue would be the distribution of property, whereas Weber felt it would be the control over bureaucracies (Mommsen, 1974). In fact, Weber argued that the nationalization of the means of production could only further alienate the workers since it would serve to extend governmental bureaucratic structures even further into the private spheres of everyday life than they might have been.

Being removed from the mainstream of activity, the aged are more affected by bureaucracy than the "inner group" of the capitalist class in America. Bureaucratization's most evident impact on the status of the aged has come about through the negation of *charisma* as a resource factor for old people in social interaction. *Charisma* was lost through the rationalization of the world that accompanied industrialization and bureaucratization and that fostered a suspicion of the spirit world, magic, and other ascientific modes of thought. The world, in effect, became demystified (Halebsky, 1976), and the locus of society's core value system, its center, moved from the sacred to the profane. The aged in traditional societies had been perceived as being closer to the sacred center of their societies because they knew the societies' traditional rituals and they were close to moving into the "new" life after death. In modern societies, however, the aged are viewed from a more clinical, detached perspective (Achenbaum, 1974). With less faith in an afterlife and weaker ties with traditional rituals, the modern world views the aged primarily in terms of their resources — that is, in terms of the rewards they can provide their exchange partners — and this rationalized perception works to the disadvantage of the aged.

Actually, it is a mistake to assume that the shift of the "center" of industrial society from sacred to profane values has left only vestiges of the mysticism that predominated during the "Before." Without question, the more sacred norms and values of our past have all but been replaced by the imperatives of abstract legal-rationalism. However, this evolution has also brought disenchantment with the world, and the interaction of these factors has had a curious result: charismatic elements of our "irrational" past remain but have been transmogrified. On the one hand, Giddens (1973, p. 275) notes "religion, magic, mysticism, become inevitably squeezed out of the organization of human conduct in the major institutional spheres of society . . . ." What has occurred, on the other hand, is that the "predominant forms of social protest (have) become utopian, futile outbursts against the imperatives of rationalization, and themselves assume a 'mystical' character." The mobilization of certain old-age organizations and movements, such as the Gray Panthers, may be better understood in this light. The image of the charismatic Maggie Kuhn waging battles against an entrenched welfare bureaucracy provides some vindication of this argument.

In addition, then, to bureaucratization and industrialization, the transition from a "traditional" to a "modern" style of life brings a decreased influence of society's "center." The center is, as Shils (1975) tells us, "not a spatially located phenomenon; rather, it is the center of the order of symbols, of values and beliefs, that govern the society" (Shils, 1975, p. 3). As modern societies move farther from their traditional centers, prestige is awarded more frequently in accordance with norms of production; occupational prestige, years of education completed, and annual income become the dominant personal resources for individuals in a rationalized world. Individuals who are not active in achievement structures (schools or labor markets) are treated with less deference than others. Thus, because of their status as retirees, old people are accorded less deference at the outset of their interaction with the middle-aged, unless they posses a counterbalancing resource.

The understanding of the dynamics of exchange relationships involving old people will not be complete as long as researchers continue to disregard historical trends. Although there still remain some "private" spheres of life that are free from outside control, Weber's fear of a future characterized by bureaucracy has, to a certain extent, been justified. In particular, the daily activities of old people are increasingly involved with establishing or maintaining relationships with bureaucratic structures. Because they are often dependent on bureaucracies for their subsistence, the aged and the poor are the groups most clearly affected by the rationalization of the modern world.

Perhaps the major problem associated with the "great transformation" to modern life is what Berger terms *deinstitutionalization*. This theme, which can be found in the writings of countless modern writers, can be summarized as the transformation of the relationship between the individual and society from a more or less harmonious state to one in which "the reciprocity between individual and society, between subjective identity and objective identification through roles, now comes to be experienced as a sort of struggle" (Berger, Berger, & Kellner, 1973, p. 218). Indeed, deinstitutionalization means that "institutions cease to be the 'home' of the self" (Berger et al., 1973). This theme is echoed by Brittan (1977) in the development of his "privatization" thesis: "there is no 'home' to be found in the political and social structures of modern society, because these structures have become 'things' outside the subjective understanding and control of individual persons" (p. 45).

In the process of deinstitutionalization and bureaucratization, the individual has lost control. The few restrictions that *are* placed on bureaucratic control are not imposed by individuals, but by "small platoons" working within mediating structures (Berger, 1975), such as the family, church, and voluntary associations. These structures are called *mediating structures* because they constitute the point of interface between the individual and increasingly remote institutions. The bureaucratic members of these remote institutions perceive an individual only as a member of a particular interest group or, simply, as a "case." The objective qualities and laws that determine an individual's social position and social relations "appear as calculable manifestations of scientific rationality" (Marcuse, 1964, pp. 168–169).

Concomitant with the decline of individual autonomy in modern society, there has occurred a discreditation of individualism as a philosophy of life. The basic components of individualism, including the beliefs in the inherent dignity of man, autonomy, privacy, and self-development, exist in the modern world in attenuated form, if at all (Lukes, 1973). In their place has emerged a counter-philosophy, the ideology of modernity. Modernity places little importance on the autonomy of individuals; instead, it emphasizes the technological superiority of modern society over previous societal forms. In this sense, modernity is an ideology. It legitimates contemporary social arrangements. The ideological aspects of modernity are captured by Tiryakian (1977) in the following definition:

> I take the term [modernity] to represent within a social order the cluster of ideational and structural elements which (a) actively supports and encourages the search for the new, that is, which provides a culture of innovations, (b) positively evaluates the contemporary arrangement of society, in terms of its internal social patterning, as well as its external adaptations to the environment, as having a legitimacy equal or superior to the 'traditional' or to previous social orders, (c) views today's social organization as an instrument to bring about tomorrow's society (rather than as an inviolate precipitate of the past, sanctified by the passage of time), and (d) considers today to be the judge of yesterday, and tomorrow to be the judge of today (rather than the reverse . . .) [p. 127].[4]

As stated, modernity is a view that legitimates contemporary institutional arrangements, and this includes the internal (within a society as opposed to between societies) distribution of society's economic surplus. In other words, modernity is an ideology that serves the interests of the elite in the inner circle of modern society—an elite that includes the core of the old capitalist class and the intellectuals and academic specialists who are situated at the core of the committees charged with policy planning for the future (cf., Bell, 1973). The groups whose interests are least served by the ideology of modernity are the working class and the aged.

The aged, more than any other age cohort, perceive modern society as distant, alien and, in some ways, oppressive. Empirical studies concerned with the effect of aging on alienation consistently show an increase in alienation from mid-life to old age. Although many of these studies justifiably point

---

[4]This and all other quotations from this source are from "The Time Perspectives of Modernity," by E. A. Tiryakian, *Society and Leisure*, 1978, *1*(1), 125–156. Copyright 1978 by Les Presses de l'Université du Québec. Reprinted by permission of the author and publisher.

to the greater disengagement of old people from role relationships as an explanation for their data, one must also recognize the ideological marginality underlying the alienation of old people.

The Coming of Post-Industrial Society

It would be futile to attempt to locate the origins of modernization and its associated ideology, modernity,[5] in a specific historical event. Modernization is part of a larger societal evolution that has its distal roots in the industrialization of America during the 19th century. Yet, at the same time, the economic and cultural expansion that followed World War II did herald a new order of rationality in modern American society. Bell's analysis of post-industrial society, for example, places the "birth years" of the new technocracy in the period between 1945 and 1950. During this period, according to Bell (1973), there appeared a new stratum in the power and privilege hierarchy. This new stratum comprises scientists and technocrats, a group whose power is based on skill and knowledge, rather than the traditional resources of strength or capital. Furthermore, according to Touraine (1971), in post-industrial society, the technocrats assume control of the power to make decisions and influence policy. As a result, the nature of class conflict changes[6]: instead of wages and profits, control over decision-making becomes the base of the conflict. For the aged and other relatively powerless groups, the transition to post-industrial society creates more distance between them and society, because these groups are not in technocratic control and thus they have nothing to do with decision-making.

The growth of modernity can be seen, then, as a historical phenomenon with a definite beginning and, therefore, a probable end. It should not be viewed, however, as an isolated development, but one that occurred within a historical dialectic. The growth of this ideology during the past thirty years has created a gradually increasing gap between traditional value systems and the reality of social life. This "reality" includes the burgeoning governmental bureaucracy, the escalation of information-related and other service industries, the instability of traditional institutions such as the church and family, and the emergent preeminence of an objective "scientific" approach to human problems. The American value "center" has, in effect, been moved, and some groups in society view this ideological shift negatively. Indeed, as I will discuss in more detail, the alienation and anomie observed among the aged and the working class are not indications of normlessness, but an indication of

[5] For additional discussion of this distinction, see Bengtson, Dowd, Smith, and Inkeles (1975).
[6] This view has also been expressed by Marcuse (1964) and other "critical" theorists, including Habermas (cited in Giddens, 1973).

rejection of the modernity ideology. This correlates with the "privatization" of life that Brittan (1977) and others have observed—the attempt of individuals to retain traditional values of individualism in their lives. Primary group life continues to exist as always; what seems to be missing, however, is the sense of linkage between daily life in neighborhoods and communities and the larger social system. Berger sums this up nicely when he distinguishes between *communal* and *abstract patriotism*. *Communal patriotism* refers to feelings of attachment to—or identification with—spatially bound, everyday physical environments, such as neighborhoods or communities. *Abstract patriotism* generalizes the feelings of communal ties to broader arenas, some of which the individual may have no direct experience with. For example, a person may identify with a particular nation or economic system without first-hand knowledge of them. Among the aged and working class, the former continues to exist; the latter, however, is becoming increasingly scarce.

The location of the loyalties of the aged and other subordinate groups within localized, or communal, networks contrasts with the modern emphasis on *mass* society. For example, Baron (1973) noted that the localized ties of groups in traditional society are "incompatible with the scale of operation, . . . [and] the calculation of self-interest that make for a viable capitalist order." Thus, what seems to be taking place is the deterioration of traditional institutions of Western Society "under the onslaught of functional rationalizing forces" (Schroyer, 1973, p. 219). Policy that was once the province of local institutions is now the responsibility of governmental agencies and private corporations. Representatives of big business have gone on record as advocating "planning" for the entire society.[7]

The convergence of many of the views discussed thus far[8] may be seen in their common concern about the accelerated movement toward technological modernism and bureaucracy that has characterized American society during the last quarter-century. Each of these writers has made the independent observation that our society is in a middle period between two epochs of longer duration. At the level of ideology, this means that optimism—including individualism and faith in the American Dream—is being replaced by a pervasive ethos of rationality, an ethos that is manifested at the policy level by the belief that social "problems" may be solved by the application of technical methods.

One result of this technocratic approach in the care of older patients is the current stress by doctors and others in the field of medicine on *cure* as opposed to *care*. For example, terminally ill aged patients need compassionate, humane care more than they need extended, frequently painful, attempts to cure their illness; however, existing technocratic attitudes prevent many

---

[7] As noted by Schroyer (1973), the advocacy of national planning by a former president of IBM was originally reported in *I. F. Stone's Weekly*, January 26, 1970.

[8] I refer here to Berger's notion of deinstitutionalization, Brittan's privatized world, Bell's concept of post-industrialized society, Marcuse's one-dimensional man, and others, including Heilbroner's civilization malaise and Nisbet's "twilight era."

professionals from adopting a humanistic approach to illness among the aged, because it seems "irrational." Because of our socialization to technical modes of thought, it seems we are less able to appreciate the limits of nature. As Schroyer (1973) noted, because of our identification with the machine, even our own bodies are becoming apperceived as technical objects.

The shift in ideology, viewed through the long lens of history, follows much the same dialectic pattern as the shift in economic forces. The shift from competitive to monopolistic capitalism, for example, eventually eroded the belief in progress and equality of opportunity that once was the major operating assumption of the American Dream. This belief system, regardless of whether it ever accurately described reality, was espoused by many Americans, if not most, as if it *were* true. It constituted, according to Tiryakian's (1977) typology, a "myth of progress." Tiryakian argues that the myth of progress is no longer held by the new middle class—the technocratic intelligentsia of the post-industrial society. Rather, it is the antithesis of the myth of progress—the ideology or myth of apocalypse or **eschaton**—that "is the one likely to achieve dominance in the emergent phase of Western modernity" (p. 17).

The notion of an oscillating, two-cycle phase of belief systems holds fascinating implications for our study of old age. As suggested by several writers, notably Foner (1974), age conflicts may arise from ideological, as well as material, reasons. I would argue that there currently exists a major ideological difference between the aged and the middle-aged generations that may best be understood in terms of the ideological evolution from a myth of progress to a myth of eschaton. Although this change may never lead to age-based social conflict between generations, it requires our attention because the social intercourse between age groups is affected by the different ideologies held by different generations.

Beginning with the 19th-century writings of the German sociologists Tönnies and Weber, one can observe how the development of the dialectic between the myths of progress and eschaton closely follows the development of major economic forces. For example, the foreboding and pessimistic visions of the German Romanticists coincides with the initial development of industrialization and constitutes an early form of the eschaton myth. This was followed by an orientation to progress, particularly in American society, that extended throughout the first half of the 20th century. The present situation, however, is one that Tiryakian notes is "marked by a steep decline in the image of the future as progress." He goes on to suggest that (1977, p. 27) it is time we consider the possibility "that Western modernity may have another cycle, that framed by an eschatological future."

If it is true that we are entering a phase dominated by a myth of eschaton, the champions of the myth are the educated elite of the new middle class. This follows the pattern—noted by Marx—in which the dominant ideas of a society are the ideas of its dominant class. It is also the dominant social groups that are the initial adherents to the ascending myth, whichever it may be. Thus, in the transitional period prior to the complete emergence of an ascending myth, elements of the subordinate classes will continue to hold to the descending belief system. In the present situation, the ascending ideology of modernity (the myth of eschaton) is more widely held among members of the dominant classes, whereas the descending ideology of individualism and the American Dream (the myth of progress) continues to be held by many of the subordinate classes, including the aged.

The measurably higher scores that older respondents score on alienation indices is consistent with this interpretation. Alienation among the aged, therefore, must not be dismissed solely as a function of the "normal" aging processes in which decreased social interaction inevitably increases one's alienation. It appears likely that this alienation may well be a reaction to the dominant ideology of modernity espoused by the ruling elite of the post-industrial society. It may be, in fact, that the alienation found among old people reflects their conscious understanding of the ideological nature of modernity; that is to say, alienation of the aged may signal old people's consciousness of the differing economic interests of the classes and the ways in which these interests are, or are not, served through belief systems such as modernity. Although most old people recognize that the American Dream's promise of social mobility will never be realized, they continue to espouse the traditional value system. Even though they may view the American Dream as a myth, most old people prefer its spirit of individual autonomy to the administered world promised by modernity.

Old Age and the Anomic Subculture

In the empirical literature focusing on the relationship between age and feelings of alienation or anomie,[9] it is generally concluded that the relationship between the two variables is curvilinear, or u-shaped. The explanation given for this finding in most cases concerns the different levels of engagement in social institutions among different age strata. The young and the old hold fewer key positions than the middle-aged in economic, political, and religious institutions and, as such, do not participate as fully in the ongoing daily life of the community. This societal marginality of the aged is presumably what is measured by the various alienation indices.

I would argue that, although this explanation for the curvilinear relationship between age and alienation is plausible, it fails to consider the

[9] Although each of these concepts has a distinct meaning, the subsequent use here of the term *alienation* will include the state of anomie. My discussion of the age/alienation relationship draws heavily from a recent paper by Dowd and Brooks (1978).

current historical context in which the alienation is observed;[10] that is, given the significant political and social changes of the 1960s, alienation no longer measures normlessness or despair—although in decades past it may have measured either or both. Instead, alienation indices today identify a population within our society that feels current institutional arrangements and social policies no longer reflect the traditional principles governing social intercourse. Values such as honesty, reliability, individualism, loyalty, and "god-fearingness" are no longer associated with the dominant social classes. The anomic subculture believes that these principles—which, they argue, allowed American society to prosper and sustained the country through the hardships of World Wars and economic depression—have been negotiated away or otherwise betrayed by the educated elite of modern society.

Alienation is, in effect, the opposite of modernity. The high degree of alienation among old people is a product of their profound dissatisfaction with the severing of modern institutions from their traditional value base. However, the standard definitions of alienation that posit a "state of mind without moral roots, standards, or sense of continuity" (MacIver, 1950) do not apply in this case. It is not the aged who have been pulled up by their "moral roots"; rather, it is *society* whose roots in traditional value systems have been severed.

Several questions must now be raised concerning the feasibility of the creation, within American society, of a class-conscious subculture that comprises disaffiliated old people and others who share the same traditional values and beliefs. The notion seems preposterous but it should be examined. The objectionable elements in this argument center on at least two points of controversy:[11] (1) If class consciousness is a representation and promotion of the economic interests of a social class, not the economic interests of an age stratum, how, then, can we speak of the *class* consciousness of *old* people? (2) If the emergence of class consciousness is a revolutionary development, how, then, can one speak of consciousness emerging from a set of values that are *traditional,* not revolutionary?

The answer to the second question is relatively straightforward, and, so, it is to this question that we turn first. The ideology of the anomic subculture (described earlier as being individualistic, personalistic, and emphasizing norms of integrity, distributive justice, and equity) is traditional in the sense that it contrasts with the prevailing ideology of modernity. This is not to say, however, that it is also simultaneously *conservative,* or an ideology

---

[10]Cutler and Bengtson's (1974) analysis of political alienation is an exception. These authors argue that the trends in political alienation during the period between 1952 and 1968 are functions of the *period effects* that occurred during this interval.

[11]Other points of controversy may exist; for example, a third possible objection may be raised to "lumping" old people and workers together in one subculture. Subcultures, of course, are not necessarily membership groups; the sine qua non of subculture is the possession of distinctive norms or other distinct cultural patterns. Our treatment of anomics as an incipiently class-conscious subculture suggests that the emergence of consciousness is the boundary between subculture and group.

in Mannheim's sense.[12] No philosophy or preferred institutional arrangement is inherently revolutionary or conservative; it only becomes so in relation to the dominant ideology. Consequently, the traditional values of the anomic subculture—given the subordinate position of the subculture vis-à-vis the dominant classes—is utopian and, as such, has a revolutionary potential.

The answer to the first question of how one relates class consciousness to age is more difficult to answer because it requires the reader to accept the possibility of an "age consciousness" and, furthermore, to recognize that, for some generational units within age strata, age consciousness and class consciousness may be the same thing. Initially, this is difficult to accept, because Marxist writers, when they discuss class consciousness, don't provide information on the ages of members of the working and ruling classes. Apparently, this information is not given because it is clearly understood that this information is *unnecessary*. It is certainly not teenagers or old people who fill the ranks of either the working or dominant classes; it is, rather, middle-aged adults who are in the majority in both classes.

The period of an individual's life from adolescence to old age is characterized by an alternating saliency of age interests and class interests (see Figure 5-1). In adolescence, the general concern is not economic conflict but generational conflict, a conflict that Bengtson and Kuypers (1971) attribute to

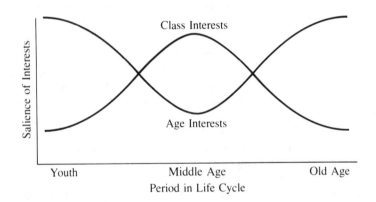

FIGURE 5-1. *Age interests and class interests in contemporary industrial society.*

[12] An ideology is a complex of ideas that functions to support or maintain the existing social order; a utopia, by contrast, is a complex of ideas that tends "to generate activities toward changes in the prevailing order" (Wirth, p. xxi in the Preface to Mannheim's *Ideology and Utopia,* 1955). Rather than analyzing historical epochs in terms of *Zeitgeist,* Mannheim argued that the world is perceived through many different orientations (reducible to ideologies or utopias). For Mannheim, there are always "simultaneous and mutually contradictory trends of thought . . . struggling against one another with their different interpretations of 'common' experience" (1936, p. 264).

the differing "developmental stakes" of youth and their parents. Youth strive for independence and autonomy whereas middle-aged parents derive greater rewards from continuity—that is, a successful transmission of their values to their offspring. The pivotal identity, or major status, of the young does not come from their economic position but their *youth;* the former has yet to be firmly established and the latter is typically believed (though, of course, mistakenly) to be a permanent distinction.

In middle age, economic competition transcends generational conflict as a dominant social force. As an adolescent, one was subordinate to the greater power (primarily economic power) and moral authority of one's parents; however, with increasing age one's independence and autonomy increases. As a consequence, the relevance of generational issues declines; those battles have been fought and resolved. The primary struggle now is economic survival.

Finally, in old age, age interests once again become dominant. Old people eventually retire from active participation in labor markets, and, equally important, age status becomes, for the first time, a permanent identity. There is no age stratum to move to after one has reached "old age." Thus, the economically based set of interests characteristic of the mid-life period undergoes drastic upheaval. In old age, age-stratum interests rather than social-class interests emerge as a factor that influences a person's identity, or consciousness.

Evidence for the claim that age consciousness and anomie are highly correlated is given in an unpublished paper that uses survey data from a representative sample of 920 residents—aged 50–80—of the Atlanta metropolitan area (Dowd, 1978a). In this paper, a measure of "belief in viability of the American system" was constructed using statements that tap the same traditional value system as the one mentioned in this chapter in relation to anomie. The statements in this index include "money has nothing to do with happiness; poor people can be just as happy as rich people" and "a person can succeed at most anything if only he or she tries hard." The point of interest here is that, although measures of socioeconomic status, such as education, occupational prestige, and the income, were significantly correlated with the system viability measure, the strongest single predictor was an index of age consciousness (beta $= +.269$).

Although class consciousness and age consciousness are separate phenomena, to the extent they describe different populations, both concepts of consciousness only have meaning in contrast to one population (the middle class, the middle aged). That is to say, working-class and aged members of the anomic subculture share a common disaffection with and, in some cases, disapprobation of the system of values known as *modernity* (Smith & Inkeles, 1966). Thus, although neither class nor age consciousness is directly measured by alienation, this conscious estrangement from the prevailing value system of modernity is precisely the referent that is being tapped by such measures as the Srole Anomia Scale.[13] This idea is in direct contrast with the view that suggests the alienated are the "poor performers in an achievement-oriented society" whose "innate intellectual capacities" render them ill equipped to "understand and assimilate societal expectations" (Otto & Featherman, 1975, p. 704). Anomie among older people should not be misconstrued to mean that the aged "do not share in the life of the articulate and active community" or that they "are prone to confusion about the norms" (McClosky & Schaar, 1965, p. 19).[14]

Old age need not be a period of life marked by alienation. This phenomenon is not the inevitable result of biological or physiological processes. It is, rather, a reaction to the loss of autonomy in our modern world. The "iron cage" of bureaucratic controls feared long ago by Weber has become a central characteristic marking the lives of old people today. However, old age, as we will discuss in the remaining sections of this book, need not be this way. Bertrand Russell understood this very well when he wrote: "old age, as I am experiencing it, could be a time of very complete happiness if one could forget the state of the world" (1969, p. 185).

Review Questions

1. Identify some of the problems or dysfunctions of bureaucracy for old people.

2. Explain the role of ideology in maintaining stratification systems.

3. Do you think the aged, like other low-status groups, have their own status symbols, or do they adopt the status symbols of the dominant strata?

4. How is the bargaining position of old people influenced by the dominant ideology of their society?

5. What is a dominant ideology? What is the dominant ideology in contemporary Western societies?

6. Max Weber argued that the key issue in the struggle of future generations will be control over bureaucracies. Marx, on the other hand, saw the distribution of property as the major issue. Considering the present situation of old people, who do you think is correct, Marx or Weber?

7. What does Shils mean by the "center"? Where is the center in modern America?

8. How do you think the coming of post-industrial society will affect old people and their relations with actors from other age groups?

[13] Srole's anomia scale attempted to measure the subjective response to a situation of structural anomie. The scale consists of five agree/disagree statements including, for example, "Most public officials are not really interested in the problems of the average man."

[14] Similar descriptions of the alienated can be found in Sniderman and Citrin (1971) and Willmuth (1976).

9. *The high anomie scores found among older people may indicate class consciousness rather than normlessness. Do you agree with this statement?*

10. *As people age, are their class interests always more important than their age interests?*

6

The Social Construction of Exchange Rates

Old age in the modern world presents to the aging individual a set of novel experiences. Much of everyday life in the latter part of the life cycle departs significantly from the commonplace activities and behavior patterns of mid-life. In the last several chapters, we have seen how the status of old people in modern societies (particularly in modern, capitalist societies) is susceptible to devaluation because of economic and ideological changes. The net result of the changes associated with modernization has been the weakening of the bargaining position of the aged in intergenerational social interaction. Specifically, because of industrial development and the development of the related ideology of modernity, it has become more difficult for old people, on the average, to negotiate favorable or, even, equitable exchange rates.

It remains to be answered, however, how the multitudinous issues involved in any exchange relationship become resolved; that is, in post-industrial society, how do individual old people and their exchange partners —particularly younger exchange partners—work out such issues as the relative "social worth" of the partners, the resources each partner possesses and is willing to exchange, the *value* of the resources to be exchanged, the *rate* at which resources are to be exchanged, and other terms of the exchange agreement? Although such terms may occasionally be submitted in written form for the approval of each partner, in most cases exchange terms are established in a much more informal manner. One example of formally established exchange terms is a marriage contract that specifically details the rights and obligations of each partner. Another example is Sussman's (1977) suggestion that old people contract with their children (in whose home they reside) for certain services to be rendered in exchange for a mutually agreeable sum of money or service. In most cases, however, approval or consent to an exchange agreement is reached through a process of informal negotiation that is commonly referred to as *conversation*.

Conversation, either in the form of language or communication through gestures and appearance, is the principal medium for the initiation, continuation, and cessation of social exchange. Although it would be a mistake to disregard the importance of historical or structural factors in a study of old age, these factors only come into play through their recapitulation in everyday conversation. That is to say, the reason modernization, for example, is of interest to social gerontologists is because of the disadvantages it imposes on the individual old person during the course of social interaction.

At this point, however, a significant parting of the ways occurs among social gerontologists concerning the conduit by which structural factors reappear in everyday social interaction. The bifurcation of opinion that I refer to here is neatly summarized by Dawe's distinction between the "two sociologies": normative sociology and interpretive sociology.[1] As I discussed in Chapter One, the *normative* tradition emphasizes the influence of social organization on human behavior. In this view, modernization is a significant social process because it affects the nature and number of social roles and normative influences that constitute human behavior in old age. Behavior, in the normative sociology, is anchored in (and bounded by) the requirements and expectations adhering to social roles, and old age in modern society becomes problematic precisely because old people are wrenched from the familiar roles of mid-life and placed in the relatively uncharted domain of old age. Behavior tends to become erratic as the normative constraints of formerly held roles recede into the past and are not replaced by others.

Interpretive sociology, by contrast, rejects the determinative link between roles and behavior hypothesized by normative sociology. Although the interpretive view agrees with role theory's view of behavior as a function of social interaction, it rejects the notion that social interaction necessarily involves two role-bounded social actors whose behavior is formed by normative constraints. Instead, interpretive sociology views social interaction as a pro-

---

[1] Dawe's work first became known to me through a paper written by Marshall (1979), in which the author applies Dawe's categories to the work of social gerontologists.

---

cess with a high degree of inherent flexibility. The outcome of an interaction is not predictable solely on the basis of the roles of the actors; rather, interaction outcomes are the result of continuous negotiations. Norms or rules may indeed emerge during the course of social interaction to give the interaction a certain "form" or regularity, but the point of contention is whether norms emerge during social interaction as factors to be taken into account or whether, as functionalists believe, they are "something 'out there' to be learned, and internalized" (Marshall, 1979, p. 348).

The exchange theory of aging as presented in this text and elsewhere (Bengtson & Dowd, in press; Dowd, 1975a) shares with both symbolic interactionism, as argued by Marshall (1979), and phenomenological sociology,[2] the belief in emergent properties. Interaction *does* involve negotiation; actors act in ways not predictable from knowledge of their roles. "Norms" are frequently violated with impunity in social interaction. In fact, behaviors that are considered "deviant" in some groups are embraced and rewarded in others. According to exchange theory, individuals tend to "interpret" rules in ways favorable to their own interests, rather than merely follow externally imposed rules.

Exchange theory also rounds out the symbolic-interactionist view of social interaction through its emphasis on power. The outcomes of interaction, although negotiable, tend nonetheless to favor the interests of the most powerful exchange partner. Roles and norms are not behavioral "straitjackets," but neither are they merely "claims" that can be discounted at will by a persuasive social actor. In fact, roles enter into the interaction process much like the status characteristics of age and sex: they are exchange resources that enhance an actor's bargaining position. For example, Torrance's (1955) famous study of three-man bomber crews shows that the person in the role of pilot influenced the decisions of those in the roles of navigator and gunner on issues completely *irrelevant* to these roles.

Without roles to give identity to the participants, interaction becomes a struggle. Social interaction normally involves an estimation by each of the actors of the relative worth of the other. This assessment is, in large part, a function of the individual's various roles, in addition to his or her status characteristics and personal resources of strength and beauty.

The emergent or spontaneous property of social interaction is clearly present in the determination of exchange rates. Exchange rates, as discussed earlier, are the outcome of negotiation in which status characteristics and other personal resources are converted into *deference* claims. Thus, the superior physical attraction or strength of one of the partners may be used to legitimate a claim to a larger share of resources. Another partner, in turn, may emphasize his or her superior educational attainments and attempt to discount the claim on this basis. The question then is: which is the superior resource—education, beauty, or another status or personal characteristic? Because of the lack of any

---

[2] See, for example, Gubrium and Buckholdt (1977).

obvious or generally accepted conversion table for translating resources into standardized *units* of power, the negotiation of identity, honor, reputation, position, or other exchange rewards is largely *unpredictable*.

The interpretive view of aging enables one to recognize the potential for creativity in dealing with the problems of aging. A creative response to human aging requires both gerontologists and old people to recognize the flexibility underlying interaction. Although old age may become a negative status characteristic in some interactions, the determination of exchange rates need not be based solely on this one criterion. Age is actually only one of an infinite variety of commodities that may be used to assess one's claim to deference and privilege. However, in order for these "other" commodities to influence the outcome of social interaction, they must be *entered* into the exchange negotiation. Unlike status characteristics like age, race, or sex, which generally become part of the negotiations automatically, those resources which are not immediately visually apparent must be *entered*. Unless exchange partners enter their own particular knowledge or experience into social interaction, the exchange rates may be set without even considering these properties as resources.

Old age, then, need not become the determinant of the social worth of an old person. It only becomes so if the old person is unable or unwilling to either define old age in positive terms or guide the negotiation to a consideration of other resources. This latter, creative alternative is needlessly absent from the normative, or role-theory, approach to aging. The role theorists stress the negative consequences of role loss that presumably befall most, if not all, of those who cross the boundary into old age. The following is a sampling of the dominant perspective in social gerontology:

> Our society does not provide major new roles for the older person. To the extent that he can hold on to pre-existent roles, he tends to retain his identity. Role demands provide a structure and sustain the motivations to keep going when one might otherwise sit back in comfort. Some people much prefer to disengage and sit back in comfort, at least for a while. Most, however, seem to remain happier and more vigorous by remaining engaged [Clausen, 1972, p. 496].

> Far too many of us shed one status only to find that there is nothing left to don. Until death. That point occurs when we enter the state of social ambiguity, of social functionlessness, of social irrelevance that is the American liminal period known as old age [Stannard, 1978, p. 11].

> Age norms can demand that people do or be something or not do or be something. They can also allow people to do certain things, but not require any specific thing. Age norms can also demand that certain choices be made [Atchley, 1975, p. 271].

The loss of roles excludes the aged from significant social participation and devalues them. It deprives them of vital functions that underlie their sense of worth, their self-conceptions and self-esteem . . . because society does not specify an aged role, the lives of the elderly are socially unstructured . . . They have no significant norms for restructuring their lives. There are no meaningful prescriptions for new goals and experience, no directions to salvation that occasionally accompany sin, loss, or failure at younger ages . . . Because they lack major responsibilities, society does not specify a role for the aged, and their lives become socially unstructured. This is a gross discontinuity for which they are not socialized, and role loss deprives them of their very social identity [Rosow, 1976, pp. 466–467].

Such statements unnecessarily imply a linkage between role incumbency and stability of self-concept and self-esteem. It is as if, once they have no roles, aged social actors become nonentities.

Furthermore, the concern with role behavior directs the researcher in his or her choice of research problems. It has become *de rigueur* among gerontologists to acknowledge the possibility that norms can "result from a negotiation process" (Atchley, 1976) or that roles do allow for considerable "role making" (Neugarten & Hagestad, 1976). Yet the steady flow of research dealing with role-related phenomena in old age belies this recent appreciation of creative behavior. If norms are truly negotiable, the focus of our research should reflect this understanding. The "diversity of response" among old people merits considerably greater attention among social gerontologists than it presently receives. Rather than continue our attempts to "fit" most old people into our reified conceptions of normal aging, we need to learn more about the ways in which older people attempt to make the most of their situations under certain social conditions.

Much discussion of timing and asynchronization, for example, has appeared in the literature recently. The conventional (normative) approach to these two topics points out that age norms are violated with greater frequency today than they were earlier. Although the life cycle can still be described as an age-linked succession of social roles (Riley, 1976), researchers have also pointed recently to the differences among age cohorts in the timing of role transitions. Neugarten and Hagestad (1976), in fact, have argued that the influence of age norms is lessening: we are moving "in the direction of an age-irrelevant society" (p. 52). Role theorists like Neugarten, when faced with data that suggest old people do not always act in ways predictable by role theory, are forced to conclude that age is apparently "diminishing in importance as a regulator of behavior" (Neugarten & Hagestad, 1976, p. 52). Rather than entertain the possibility that role theory may not be the most appropriate lens with which to view the aging process, role theorists conclude, instead, that age is no longer important as a behavioral "regulator." Thus, although lipservice is obligingly paid to the notions of "negotiation" and "role making," in the final analysis, the world of the role theorist is still one in which behavior is *regulated*. Roles, norms, and social order are still the major conceptual categories of gerontological theorists.

From the alternative "interpretive" perspective, a concept such as asynchronization is not treated as a reified category; "timing" and similar definitions of appropriate movement in a career are not generalizable phenomena. The observation that people frequently engage in behaviors that are linked with a different age grade does not necessarily lead to the conclusion that age is becoming irrelevant. In fact, age remains relevant as a resource in social interaction. Indeed, the demographic transition in America to an older population seems certain to make age an increasingly important factor in theories of social behavior. What *is* becoming irrelevant is the belief that behavior in old age (and at other points in the life cycle) is determined by social roles. From the interpretive perspective, the interesting point concerning asynchronization is the way in which definitions of appropriate "timing" are constructed by individuals in their social interactions. There may not be a single definition shared by all actors in the interaction; in cases where there is not, the definition of appropriate timing or speed is negotiated. As in most interaction, the outcome—the emergent definition—will depend upon the relative power of the actors involved.

Socialization Processes in Old Age

Socialization *is* social interaction. Just as social interaction transforms the "mewling, puking infant" into the sophisticated student who sat before George Herbert Mead, the identity of old people is also shaped through the interaction process. It is not shaped, however, through the learning of age norms or other "socialization contents" that exist, somehow, apart from the actual social interaction itself. Old-age socialization, however, is not an assembly-line process in which an old person is fashioned from the whole cloth of middle age; rather, the process is more appropriately conceptualized as a series of interactions between the individual and others in his or her environment—the outcome of which is neither predictable nor inevitable.

Contrasting research on the lives of old people in different groups documents the various ways the aged in American society meet the challenge of daily life in creative and, from the viewpoint of middle-aged society, sometimes deviant ways. For example, the "bag lady" described by Curtin (1972), although isolated and poor, managed to maintain a sense of autonomy and dignity through use of her particular resource: a presentation of herself as being crazy. So, too, in Stephens' (1974; 1975) analyses of life in a rundown SRO (Single Room Occupancy) hotel in Detroit, we learn of how the older residents sustain the dominant norms of the SRO (privacy, autonomy, and utilitarianism) in an effort to achieve a sense of control over their environment. Similar accounts of the emergence of new roles in other settings and accompanying "notions of the right and wrong of them" are given by Hochschild (1973) and Seguin (1973). Each of these studies suggests the futility of attempting to predict the relative "success" of any socialization effort without extensive knowledge of the values and the distribution of power resources within the group to be socialized. Since all socialization is a process of "bilateral negotiation" (Bengtson & Black, 1973), the outcome of the process is a function of (1) the relative power of the actors involved and (2) the "meanings" each of the actors attributes to the matter under negotiation.

The exchange/symbolic-interactionist view is undeniably optimistic about the ability of old people to construct their own social worlds in ways favorable to themselves. Although it would be difficult to argue against the reality of role loss in old age, we need to be more critical of the role theorists' conclusion that role loss and personal disintegration are necessarily linked. A healthy departure from this "conventional wisdom" can be observed in a recent paper by Huyck (1978). She argues that most old people are not "victims" who are

> propelled into crisis after crisis by role losses, illness, and relocation. Nor are old people the 'victims' of their own internal disintegration, inevitably losing cognitive abilities and withdrawing interest and energy from the outside world. Rather, adaptive capacities remain as potentials residing in the mutual interaction of self and surrounds [p. 13].

The adaptive capacities of old people were observed by Hochschild (1973) in her frequently cited study of old women residing in an apartment building. The residents were not unique, nor was the apartment building noticeably special. Yet the description Hochschild gives of the residents' lives certainly is not one that would be predicted on a role-theory perspective. Hochschild captures the creative ways in which these women are making their way through the life cycle:

> For old roles that are gone, new ones are available. If the world watches them less for being old, they watch one another more. Lacking responsibilities to the young, the old take on responsibilities toward one another. Moreover, in a society that raises an eyebrow at those who do not "act their age," the subculture encourages the old to dance, to sing, to flirt, and to joke. They talk frankly about death in a way less common between the old and young. They show one another how to be, and trade solutions to problems they have not faced before [1973, p. 141].[3]

From this passage, one can see the individualized or autonomous side of human behavior. Although it is certain that roles and norms constitute the "building blocks" of social organization (as introductory sociology textbooks invariably point out), one should not lose sight of the fact that social structure

[3] This and all other quotations from this source are from *The Unexpected Community*, by A. R. Hochschild. Copyright 1973 by Prentice-Hall, Inc. Reprinted by permission.

exists only through social interaction; that is, it exists only as long as the participants in an exchange relationship continue to view certain status characteristics as worthy of certain rewards. If, for whatever reasons, the value attributed to a certain status characteristic—or other personal resource—changes, the interaction pattern will also change. In this process, the social structure itself is transformed.

Old people, as long as they remain active participants in social exchange relationships, have the power to affect social interactions and, ultimately, social structure. The key to this remarkable source of power is, simply, *talk*. Deference is shown or withheld during the course of *conversations*. However, the mere possession of a power resource is insufficient, in most cases, to obtain a share of privilege. The resource must be activated during the course of social interaction in order for the individual's claim to be accepted as legitimate. Talk is the means by which potential power is converted into power-in-use.

Listening to people and understanding the meaning of their words is, in essence, an act of obedience. As we listen to someone speak, we give up consciousness of our own identities if only for a brief second, in order to translate that person's words into metaphors that relate to our own experience. To "listen," then, is actually to "obey" the command of language (Jaynes, 1976). The problem language presents for the individual engaged in conversation is its limitation, or control, of such obedience. One way this works, according to Jaynes, is through *opinions*. For example, in order to reduce a person's voice-authority over us, we must disesteem that person. Thus, the same words spoken by different people may not be received by us in the same way. Because we hold different speakers in different levels of esteem, the words they speak are accorded different degrees of credence. In response to the question why we are "forever judging, forever criticizing, forever putting people in categories of faint praise or reproof," Jaynes responds that we do so in order to regulate other people's control over us and our thoughts: "Our personal judgments of others are filters of influence. If you wish to release another's language power over you, simply hold him higher in your own private scale of esteem" (1976, p. 98).

Another aspect of interpersonal relationships that requires our attention is the *situational context* in which interactions occur. By this I mean that exchange relationships that are *not* restricted to a particular situational context (the work place, for example) require renegotiation of the exchange rate in each situation. So, for example, when two actors who have established an exchange relationship in the context of work decide to continue their association apart from work, a new exchange rate may have to be negotiated to cover the new aspect of their relationship. Although the partner who is more powerful in the work context may attempt to establish his or her hegemony in the new situation, there is no reason why this has to be so. Of course, the resources that enabled one partner to achieve the advantage in the work context may also be operative in the new situation. Or, the partner with the initial advantage may attempt to *convince* the other actor that the superior nature of his or her resources extends to the present context as well.[4]

In any case, power must continually be used if an actor wishes to obtain a favorable outcome from a particular interaction. There is no guarantee that all interactions between the same exchange partners will always have the same outcome; a favorable outcome in one case does not guarantee— although it makes it more likely —a favorable outcome in a later interaction. This is particularly true if, as mentioned previously, the situational context has been changed or modified. So, for example, actor A may defer to actor B in the context of their interactions on the job; yet, when A and B decide to play golf on weekends, the relationship may change.

As we have seen, the medium through which exchange relationships are established and maintained is some form of talk, or conversation. The grandmother in Edward Albee's (1961) play *The American Dream* is fully aware of this. Her status within the family has changed as she has grown old; she no longer is deferred to by others in everyday conversation, and, thus, her status has been devalued. After one particularly unpleasant exchange, she observes the following:

> I suppose I deserve being talked to that way, I've gotten so old. Most people think that when you get so old, you either freeze to death, or you burn up. But you don't. When you get so old, all that happens is that people talk to you that way [p. 19].

Actors have a variety of means open to them to convey their esteem or contempt for their exchange partners. Communication through facial gestures, for example, is frequently used to convey a sense of superiority, disapproval, keen interest, or a wide assortment of other attitudes. When a third party is present, he or she may be used by one of the actors as a participant in a deference ritual, or what Goffman (1959) terms a *team performance*. A sly wink, a knowing glance, or a raising of the eyebrows may be used to convey approval or disapproval from one exchange partner to the third party. Other communication techniques include interrupting the partner, talking more loudly than the partner, looking past the other person while speaking to him or her, or initiating new avenues of conversation to maintain the interest of the partner.

Control over, or manipulation of, the actual content of the conversation is, therefore, perhaps the most important criterion for establishing the legitimacy of one's claim to a share of available rewards. Although one's need to control conversations declines as one's power increases, some form of conversation always accompanies the accumulation of privilege.

---

[4]For more information on the relationship between conversation and social behavior, see Hall and Hewitt (1970); Hewitt and Hall (1973); Hewitt and Stokes (1975); Scott and Lyman (1968); and Stokes and Hewitt (1976).

Conversation is also important in establishing reputations, which, in turn, play a role in the control one may have over the conversation. A person's status within a group may be manifested in terms of *reputation*—the group's generalized estimate of the person's worth. Reputations, however, are not the property of individuals, something that can be stored in a safe place and preserved. A reputation is a property of social interaction; that is, it exists only when two or more people refer to it during the course of conversation. Reputations can also be modified—enhanced or ruined—through talk. Gossip, for example, is an effective means of social control because it directly affects reputations, which are the measure of a person's social standing.

This facet of social status is important to recognize if we wish to know what happens to the individual social actor as he or she ages. If, because of the steadily decreasing profits associated with an exchange relation, older people choose to disengage from relations, they become more vulnerable to the negative talk (labeling) of others. When disengaged old people no longer participate in particular exchange relations, the probability increases that they will also not be present at these interactions to defend their reputations. In such cases, the missing person's reputation stands to be "reinterpreted" by the remaining exchange members, and so the social status of this person may be altered.

Thus, we can see that merely behaving in a certain way or committing a particular act is insufficient to ruin a person's reputation or lower someone's status. In order to affect a person's reputation or status, the act must be discussed and the actors involved must mutually decide whether the performance in question is "deviant." Frequently, if the "offending" party is sufficiently powerful, the "offense" may be interpreted as justifiable under the circumstances. Politicians accused of unethical or illegal behavior may not be condemned by their constituents, but defended as targets of unscrupulous "enemies."

The status-conferring role of conversations is discussed in considerable detail by Collins (1975):

> Generally speaking, all talk is negotiation. . . . Conversation creates subjective realities, and it also creates social relationships. What is being negotiated . . . includes the cognitive reality of the moment and the personal relationships among the conversationalists. . . . Much of the bargaining is tacit, as people negotiate what kind of a relationship they will have and what kind of reality they will enact. Not all of it is tacit or symbolic, however. Practical talk, at some point, includes overt negotiations about the material benefits of the deal [p. 114]. . . . Conversation is an exchange. . . . all of these exchanges may be regarded as ways of getting interpersonal status—resources through which one may optimize the amount of deference and support he gets from others [p. 133].

Conversations, then, are the principle means of showing or withholding deference, and, as such, they constitute the mechanism by which power is converted into privilege. The ability to converse well, however, is not distributed equally among all members in an exchange network. One's ability to negotiate positive results in social interaction is related to one's resources —command of the language spoken within the group and the ability to communicate clearly, for example—as well as one's status characteristics. Words spoken by a middle-aged male, for example, may have a more positive effect on an exchange group than the same words spoken by an old woman. One of the reasons this is so is simply because exchange partners are willing to show a more powerful partner greater deference than they would show a less powerful partner for the same resource or investment. In other words, power begets power. In the case of conversation, words are given different meanings and values depending upon the relative status of the person who utters them.

This power differential is certain to make inter-generational exchanges unrewarding, at times, for the aged partner. Even in everyday, mundane types of social interaction—such as a routine conversation between an old man and his son—power is being used, and the relative status and position of the actors vis-à-vis each other are undergoing gradual but significant modification. The partner who is more powerful can control the interchange by controlling the conversation. Suggestions may be made during conversations that hold negative implications for the reputation of one partner. Unless that partner has the ability (through possession of personal resources) to contradict these negative suggestions, they may become part of the memories and identities of each partner as the "new reality." In subsequent conversations, the "injured" partner must introduce new information (or reintroduce old but still valuable information) if he or she wants to return to the "old reality" and vindicate his or her reputation. To do this, however, the injured partner needs power resources, but it was the lack of these resources that led to the devaluation of his or her reputation in the first place. Consequently, social interactions often tend to proceed (in the short run) consistently, with one partner consistently gaining—and the other partner consistently losing—privilege and prestige.[5]

An example of differential ability in controlling social interactions is given in a recent analysis of family relationships by Dowd and LaRossa (1978). In this paper, the authors observed a *negative* correlation between the frequency of older, dependent males' contact with their children and the older males' level of morale. That is to say, for those older men (aged 65 to 80) who were relatively dependent on their children for reasons of income or health, the more contact they had with their children, the lower their morale was. The authors explain this surprising finding in terms of a shift in the balance of power between the older male and his adult children that occurs during the period following the older male's retirement. Retirement redefines not only the retiree's labor-force status but also his status within the family. Because he no longer holds a job, the retiree loses an important status characteristic for his

---

[5]This is the short-run cycle. In the long run, if the less powerful partner is able to withstand the devaluation and maintain the relationship, the exchange will tend toward a balanced position.

relatives to defer to, and thus he no longer has a claim to the same share of privilege and prestige that he used to have within the family.

However, even if an older male retiree loses status, why should a visit from one of his adult children be associated with a decline in his morale? The answer lies in the fact that the renegotiation of an exchange relationship —such as the one between a dependent older male and his middle-aged son—occurs during social interaction. Specifically, status renegotiations are worked out through conversations. Thus, the frequent visits from the middle-aged son or daughter constitute the occasions or situations during which a role reversal is negotiated.[6] Although the purpose of the visits and the content of the conversations during the visit may belie this point, the visits actually involve a ritual that has been performed in various guises as long as parents have survived to witness their children's emergence as adults. The ritual is one in which the older parent, especially the older male, "cedes control" of the family (and, hence, his own future) to his progeny. This ritual is very costly for the older male and brings with it few, if any, rewards. Consequently, the visits from his adult children lower his morale.

The drama of generational succession, in which control is transferred from a descending to an ascending generation, constitutes a *rite de passage* —albeit an ambiguous one—into old age. Like no other single event, its occurrence signals the decline of prestige and status of the older individual. In our social exchanges, each of us desires—perhaps more than any other reward —a degree of deference that allows us to sustain a positive image of our own worth. Although some individuals are able to maintain a healthy self-concept even during long stretches without supportive human contact, in most cases, social interaction is necessary to build self-esteem. Consequently, one of the major agreements to be worked out in any social exchange is the manner in which each of the partners will aid the other in attaining a positive sense of self. Collins (1975) views friendship relations, for example, as consisting of the bargain: "I'll provide a sympathetic audience for your recapitulation of the events of your recent experience, if you'll do the same for me" (p. 114). On a larger scale, Collins views social relationships as "rituals in which participants work together to uphold an idealized reality" (1975, p. 162). It is my position that much of the anguish associated with growing old is caused by the loss of precisely these opportunities to engage in "team performances." In general, the social exchanges that characterize old age do not permit the older person to uphold his or her idealized image of self. Instead, old people are frequently placed in situations in which they have little choice but to internalize the negative labels imposed on them by others.[7]

---

[6]The concept of a generational "role reversal" has been argued previously by Sussman (1976). The negotiation of this reversal marks the beginning of the last phase of the parent/child relationship—the single most important exchange relation in the life of an individual.

[7]The insightful analysis by Kuypers and Bengtson (1973) of the "social breakdown syndrome" provides a detailed account of how the process of negative internalization works in old age.

The lack of opportunities to "enact cherished role identities" (McCall & Simmons, 1966, p. 158) may account in part for the level of anger and emotional expressiveness observed among some old people (Myerhoff, 1975). All people, regardless of age, require validation of their self-worth by significant others. For many people, social interaction with close friends and family members provides the opportunity for validation. When deprived of this opportunity, however, people may seek to confirm their basic value and dignity in ways that *require* others in the immediate environment to recognize them. Because of the relative scarcity of legitimate opportunities to publicly reconfirm their self-worth, old people may choose to employ intrusive strategy, such as making a "scene" by violating the tacit rules governing social intercourse (asking embarrassing questions, for example, or responding with great detail to a question not intended to gain information).

The disengagement that characterizes many old people (I am referring not to the "voluntary" disengagement discussed by Cumming and Henry, but to the decreased social interaction and "shrinking lifespace" that is precipitated by retirement or the loss of family members through relocation) places them in a situation characterized by an acute shortage of reliable information. Other people, as Charles Horton Cooley (1912) observed years ago, are the major sources of information concerning the presentation of our "public" selves. Lacking such sources, old people may find themselves in very vulnerable positions in which they must actively solicit information from other people.

The degree of difficulty old people face in their attempts to obtain reliable information about their status within their exchange networks increases exponentially in relation to the degree to which their exchange partners (family members, for example) begin to view them or their "situations" as *problems*. When their grown children begin to discuss their adaptation to retirement (or failure to adapt), for example, old people will be informed less about their actual status in the family, and the nature of the interaction between the old parents and their adult children will begin to change. The children monitor their parents' behavior, looking for signs of deterioration or other evidence of maladaptation. Old people, sensing this, may attempt to retain the level of deference their children previously showed them by *limiting* the amount of information about their health or state of mind that they give to their children. They may, in fact, decide to withhold from them any information that may be interpreted to mean a loss of personal resources and that may then be used as evidence to justify a renegotiation of exchange rates.

Viewed in this light, old age is remarkably similar to paranoia. Like the paranoid person, the old man or woman is placed in a special status; people react to the person and interpret his or her behavior in terms of this special status. Oftentimes people enter into conspiracies against the person in order to protect group values or to insure that the routine social interaction within the group will not be interrupted by the person. Family members may conspire, for example, to commit an aged person to a hospital or a nursing home. And, like the paranoid person, old people may adopt a strategy of aggressive or hostile behavior in order to assert their self-worth, to provoke an incident and thereby obtain needed information, or to ascertain the "dimension and form of the coalition arrayed against" them (Lemert, 1962, p. 14).[8]

Lemert's brilliant analysis of the social dynamics underlying paranoia holds much relevance for the study of old age. I do not, however, intend to suggest that old age in any way represents a paranoid period of life or that paranoia is more characteristic of the old than the young. The similarity between paranoia and old age lies in the way in which old people and paranoids are often susceptible to organized conspiratorial activity and other singular treatment. Meacher argues, for example, that "confusion" among old people is not an endogenous condition but a "system of 'logical' adjustments to a mystifyingly insecure and alarming environment" (1972, p. 280).

Lemert's accounts of the process of defining the paranoid person as "paranoid" also describe the process of defining the recent retiree as "old" or the "old" person as "senile":[9]

> Although the paranoid person reacts differentially to his social environment, it is also true that 'others' react differentially to him, and this reaction commonly, if not typically, involves covertly organized action and conspiratorial behavior in a very real sense [p. 3]. The paranoid process begins with persistent interpersonal difficulties that frequently or even typically arise out of bona fide or recognizable issues centering upon some actual or threatened loss of status for the individual [p. 7]. The behavior of the individual—arrogance, insults, presumption of privilege, and exploitation of weaknesses in others—initially has a segmental or checkered pattern in that it is confined to status-committing interaction. Outside of these, the person's behavior may be quite acceptable —courteous, considerate, kind, even indulgent. . . . In the early generic period, tolerance by others for the individual's aggressive behavior . . . is broad, and it is very likely to be interpreted as a variation of normal behavior . . . at some point . . . a new configuration takes place in perceptions others have of the individual. . . . From a normal variant the person becomes 'unreliable,' 'untrustworthy,' 'dangerous,' or someone with whom others 'do not wish to be involved.' . . . Once the perceptual reorientation takes place, either as the outcome of continuous interaction or through the receipt of biographical information, interaction changes qualitatively . . . it becomes *spurious*, distinguished by patronizing, evasion, 'humoring,' guiding conversation onto selected topics, underreaction, and silence—all calculated either to prevent intense interaction or to protect individual and group values by restricting access to them. When the interaction is between two or more persons in the

[8] This and all other quotations from this source are from "Paranoia and the Dynamics of Exclusion," by E. M. Lemert, *Sociometry*, 1962, *25*, 2–20. Copyright 1962 by the American Sociological Association. Reprinted by permission of the author and publisher.

[9] The *social construction* of senile identities is the theme of several other sociological monographs dealing with the subject of mental illness in old age. Included among these are Frankfather (1977); Gubrium (1978); Meacher (1972); and Wershow (1977).

individual's presence, it is cued by a whole repertoire of subtle expressive signs that are meaningful only to them [p. 8].

Once the battle is won by the exclusionists, their version of the individual as dangerous becomes a crystallized rationale for official action. At this point misrepresentation becomes part of a more deliberate manipulation of ego . . . for example, to get him to submit to psychiatric examination . . . preliminary to hospital commitment [p. 14].

The elderly who are most susceptible to being labeled as sick, senile, incompetent, or useless are those with the fewest resources and the least power. Since negative labels are imposed during conversations, old people whose resources enable them to participate in conversations with younger persons are in the position to construct different and more positive identities for themselves than old people who are disengaged from social interaction. Old people with few resources and little power, however, are the ones most likely to be disengaged. Thus, the poor elderly, for example, are admitted to hospitals as mental incompetents with a frequency disproportionate to their numbers (Markson, 1974). Lack of power is also the major reason why some old people are vulnerable to the Social Breakdown Syndrome. To explain this vulnerability one must go beyond the observations of old age "rolelessness and normlessness" (Kuypers & Bengtson, 1973). The social breakdown suffered by some old people can be traced to the decreased social interaction that accompanies old age and that creates an information deficit and increased dependence on external cues.

When one discusses these and similar issues with students or colleagues, one question that invariably is asked concerns the emotional bond between generations. Doesn't the "role-reversal" process imply a lack of love or affection between the generations? How could middle-aged sons and daughters conspire to denigrate the people who raised and nurtured them from birth? One answer to these questions involves a denial of the ritual of "ceding control": according to some, in those families where love abounds, the old person is not subjected to this devaluation.

These questions, however, raise a complex and significant problem —one which makes the discussion of intergenerational family relationships more than just a point of academic interest. Does the process of role reversal create emotional disharmony within the older person's family? Some writers discount completely the applicability of emotional ties between generations. According to these writers, the relationship between generations is ruled by rational self-interest:

The characteristic mark of the adult's attitude towards the old is its duplicity. Up to a certain point, the adult bows to the official ethic of respect for the aged that has, as we have seen, asserted itself during the recent centuries. But it is in the adult's interest to treat the aged man as an inferior being and to convince him of his decline. He does his best to make his father aware of his deficiencies and blunders so that the old man will hand over the running of his affairs, give up advising him, and submit to a passive role. Although the pressure of public opinion forces the son to help his old parents, he means to rule them as he sees fit. . . .

It is in an underhand, sly manner that the adult tyrannizes over the dependent old man. . . . Naturally, he always says he is acting in the old man's own interest. The whole family abets him. The old man's resistance is worn down; . . . they treat him with ironic kindness, talking in childishly simple terms and even exchanging knowing winks over his head. . . . The wife and the boy who are dependent on the adult can defend themselves better than the old man: the wife renders service—bed-service and the housework—and the boy will grow into a man capable of calling the adult to account; the old man will do nothing but travel downwards to decrepitude and death. He is a mere object, useless and in the way [de Beauvoir, 1972, p. 218].

A similar view is presented by Anderson (1972). She argues that the problematic existence of old people makes us uncomfortable. In order to cope with the discomfort, we attempt to exclude them from our social interactions and, if possible, banish them to nursing homes, where their exclusion can be total:

With a discontinued world, the old have become social phantoms, and, like phantoms, they make us uncomfortable. We relegate them to white-sheeted habitats where they (and we) feel more comfortable among their own kind; we send them to golden-age homes, antechambers to eternity [p. 212].

Although the analyses of Anderson and de Beauvoir may accurately describe the family relationships of some old people, their views are excessively pessimistic. Many old people remain integral members of family networks, either living under the same roof as their children or within an "intimate" distance. Others choose a life apart from their children, preferring to live either alone or among age peers. And, in the many cases of role reversal, in which power is transferred between generations, the process is rarely characterized by bitter recrimination or disaffection. Because the ritual of ceding control is mandated by our culture, its legitimacy is rarely questioned. Although the morale of the old person may decline in the process, the love and concern shared by both parents and children probably remain constant in most cases. The exercise of power in social relationships is, I should emphasize, a function of the possession of power, not of a deficient or aggressive personality. The mere possession of power resources guarantees their use. Consequently, power is exercised in all social relationships, regardless of the nature of the emotional bonds between the partners.

Review Questions

1. Explain what is meant by the "social construction of exchange rates."
2. What is the likelihood that an age-conscious group of older Americans will

emerge in the next 50 years? With what types of issues would such a group be concerned?

3. Discuss the functions of talk in determining exchange rates.
4. Why is socialization a never-ending process, continuing throughout life?
5. In what sense can we say that cross-age relations involve "boundary crossings"?
6. Describe the process of role reversal as this concept applies to generational relations.
7. In what sense is retirement a rite of passage?
8. Old age is remarkably similar to paranoia. Do you agree with this statement?

7

Some Thoughts about Social Policy

*The Delivery of Services
to the Aged*

The state of the world, as Bertrand Russell noted, is a difficult matter to dismiss. Society may wish to abandon old people, and old people may wish to disengage themselves from the world, but neither occurrence is either completely possible or desirable. Although complete disengagement would have undesirable consequences for old people, I do not mean to suggest that disengagement should be combatted by legions of geriactivists, whose function it would be to persuade—indeed require—old people to *participate*. Although they are well-intentioned, such activists usually do not care about the *mode* of participation; they usually care only that old people keep themselves *busy*. Although it is not particularly innovative, their message is clear: STAY ACTIVE!

I am of the opinion that we could use less, not more, of the paternalistic pigheadedness that spawns such notions. The "state of the world" that infiltrates most corners of the everyday lives of the aged is a bureaucratized, service-providing, help-delivering, problem-solving, "jointly-sponsored" program managed by a growing network of agencies and institutions, both governmental and private. The product delivered in many cases is, to be sure, welcomed by the old person, because it is truly needed. At the same time, however, the mode of delivery often serves to produce a continued state of dependency and sense of ineffectiveness on the part of old people.

This complaint about the delivery of services to the aged bears repetition, because the conditions that originally caused it have not improved. I refer specifically to the misguided belief among professionals in the field of gerontology that our "knowledge" of aging processes renders us fit to prescribe for old people what behaviors are for their "own good." Although this "paternalistic assertion" (Halper, 1978) may, in some cases, be justified, its net effect in the large majority of cases is deleterious. Even if paternalistic intervention "solves" some short-term problems, it also serves to further increase the dependency of old people, which, in the long run, will damage their morale and self-esteem.

Social Policy and the Independence of the Aged

The origins of the "paternalistic assertion" that the aged are in "need of substantial outside help, whether they know it or not" (Halper, 1978, p. 323), probably lie in the modernity syndrome and, specifically, in the faith of modern technocrats in bureaucratic procedures and scientific "human engineering." The emphasis, as Weber pointed out several decades ago, is on total administrative control. The lives of old people in institutionalized settings are especially vulnerable to the workings of this philosophy. It has been noted by Halper, for example, that "the bureaucratic imperative of manageability is often sought through such products of science as the drug thorazine, which facilitates custodial care by numbing the elders. . . ." One particularly unnerving aspect of the bureaucratic perspective is its "catch-22" clause, which presumes that all those who resist the help or refuse the services of the geriactivist are, ipso facto, in the greatest need of all.

This perspective fails to realize, of course, that disengagement or preference for solitary activities may constitute the most rational course of action under the circumstances. Rather than suggesting the possibility of psychological malfunctioning (paranoia, for example), such behavior may indicate the older person's firm resolve to retain his or her independence for as long as possible. In her excellent analysis of the behavior of old people who attended one particular senior center, Matthews (1977) argues that the decision of many of the participants to withdraw from the center was a tactic they employed to remain autonomous. Those who disengaged were not merely "giving up" or leaving because they were the "poor performers" in an active society and could no longer bear the burden of "performance." Rather, Matthews argues, the decision to leave was calculated—that is, based on a serious evaluation of the rewards and costs involved. Instead of enduring the costs of continued interaction with the center's middle-aged staff—who viewed them primarily as "old" and, therefore, dependent—these old people decided to eliminate the costs altogether (and the rewards as well) by "leaving the field." Matthews observes that the strategy of "negotiation by default" was "one way for the old to protect their self-images," a means "to avoid interaction with others who will respond to their oldness as pivotal."

From an exchange theory perspective, the behavior described by Matthews is rational, since the older person who "defaults" recognizes the fact of declining profits and takes steps to rebalance the exchange. Blau (1964a) includes the strategy of withdrawal as one of the options available to the dependent exchange partner to rebalance a particular relationship. Although this option is chosen only very infrequently because of the actor's continued need for rewards, the decision to withdraw or disengage is probably the best alternative, given an understanding of the critical importance of independence in most people's lives. It is a decision, in any case, that old people themselves are in the best position to make. The wishes of the geriactivist that old people remain active notwithstanding, the old person who decides to withdraw *must* be granted this right without being labeled "disorganized" or "irrational." Researchers have documented this point in recent studies. Lowenthal and Robinson (1976), for example, state that "ranking low in network involvement at any life-stage does not necessarily result in low morale or poor mental health or whatever measure we wish to use."

Once we establish the essential importance of autonomy in the lives of old people, much of their behavior can be understood as a continuing effort to maintain their independence in the face of a world intent upon total administration. In fact, one might argue (as I would) that old people—indeed, people of all ages—live out their everyday lives with an implicit understanding of the rules of social exchange, particularly the inverse relationship between power and dependence. Although academicians attempting to build reliable theories may frame their explanations in words that occasionally confuse more than clarify, the reality their words intend to convey is understood only too well by most old people.

Consequently, our gerontological literature is filled with disparate studies pointing to a similar conclusion that are without a unifying framework to focus their common concerns. We know, for example, that the aged in rural areas are reluctant to accept help, particularly if it requires a public declaration of poverty (Moen, 1978). We also know that the concern with death that characterizes older women is not necessarily a *fear* of death; rather, it is a fear of the dying *process* that "centers on 'suffering' and 'being a burden,' both of which fall under the category of losing control over self-identity" (Matthews, 1975, p. 108). The "intimacy-at-a-distance" style of intergenerational family contact is another pertinent example of the aged's struggle to maintain control over their lives. So, too, is Blenkner's observation that:

Most older persons under 75 are quite capable of taking care of themselves and their affairs. They neither want nor need to be 'dependent,' but they do want and need someone to depend on, should illness or other crisis arise [1965, p. 53].

This central fact of life in old age—the struggle to remain independent —must become the guiding principle of future policies and plans regarding old people. This does not mean that we should adopt a plan whereby the old person is cut off from social support and forced to rely upon what social workers euphemistically refer to as "personal support systems." Rather, it means that we should attempt to maximize the autonomy of old people by carefully considering the two themes implicit in the preceding quote from Blenkner: individualism and community support (gemeinschaft or primary group could easily be substituted for "community"). Although individualism may appear inconsistent with the concept of *gemeinschaft* (a group-oriented social organization characterized by small size, face-to-face contact, and personal ties), the two concepts need not be mutually exclusive. They are, rather, two principles, neither one of which should be disregarded in the planning of policy.

Individualism is not used here as a code word for a reactionary policy of governmental laissez-faire. An investigation of the historical uses of the term reveals that the basic ideas of individualism include notions of the *dignity of man, autonomy, privacy,* and *self-development.*[1] Each of these components of individualism, however, is threatened by bureaucratic control and the cultural hegemony of modern capitalism. They are also sadly missing in our prevailing policies regarding the aged and our everyday social interactions with them. If we want to prevent a future escalation of generational conflict as our economic growth rate stabilizes and/or declines, we must become committed to the principle of individual autonomy. This commitment requires that we view old people not as a group defined as needing *our* help, but as active agents in the management of their own lives.

Saying that we must make this commitment is, of course, much easier than doing it. The task of altering the prevailing view of the aged will be difficult, because our stratified social structure relegates old people to a subordinate position in the hierarchy. Consequently, if we are seriously concerned with the independence of our old people, we must be committed at the same time to reducing the inequalities among age groups in our society. The difficulties this entails are noted by Lukes:

thus, for example, one will need to look very closely at the structural determinants of status ranking, if one is concerned to increase equality, or at the

[1]According to Lukes' (1973) careful analysis, the historical referents for these ideas range widely from the New Testament to Kant, Luther, Calvin, Spinoza, St. Thomas Aquinas, Herbert Marcuse, 19th-century German Romanticists, and Karl Marx.

deeper influences (for example, through language and perception) of the agencies of socialization, if one is concerned to maximize autonomy and self-development [1973, p. 157].[2]

One thing that we can do to increase the independence of the aged in American society is to abolish mandatory retirement policies. Although the age of mandatory retirement has changed recently from 65 to 70, any predetermined judgment of the occupational competence of a worker that is based on age is discriminatory, pure and simple. Evaluation of competence should be based on performance, not age. Those who present arguments *for* mandatory retirement tend to disregard the economic burdens imposed on old people in particular, and families in general, by inflation, the moral problems involved in any form of systematic discrimination, and the problems such a policy would impose on individuals attempting to negotiate equitable exchange rates.[3] Sheppard (1976) accounts for recent signs of a trend toward late retirement in terms of the high inflation rate of the 1970s and the prospects for its continuation.

Old people themselves can aid their cause through the recognition —and greater appreciation—of the power they *do* possess. It has been frequently observed, for example, that old people oftentimes contribute more to their adult children than they receive (Streib & Streib, 1978). And Shanas (1967) notes that middle- and working-class older men report that they have helped their children more often than the reverse. In the context of exchange theory, this pattern of giving more than receiving indicates that the power advantage in the relationship favors the middle-aged receiver. The exchange rate, in this case, may be something like two or three units of help from the aged parent for every one unit of help from the middle-aged child. The old person in this case is obviously more dependent on the rewards he or she obtains from the exchange than is the younger exchange partner—hence, the unbalanced rate of exchange. Rosenmayr (1977) similarly notes this unbalanced state when he writes (p. 135): "there is some evidence that parent/adult-child relations are not fully reciprocal; inasmuch as aged parents seem more attached to their children than children to parents."

Old people need to recognize the inherent value of the resources they exchange in their relations with their children. In unbalanced exchanges, it would be a mistake for old people to assume that a gift or loan to an adult child necessarily builds an account that they may "call in" when they are in need of assistance (cf., Streib & Streib, 1978). Instead, the gift may be defined (in the context of an unbalanced exchange) as the middle-aged child's privilege—a commodity that is *expected* under the implicit rules governing the exchange.

[2] This and all other quotations from this source are from *Individualism* by S. Lukes. Copyright © by Basil Blackwell Publisher Ltd.
[3] The case for mandatory retirement has been argued many times by academicians and businesspersons. One recent attempt, unsuccessful in my view, is by Creighton (1978).

Understanding this, old people would be in a better position to realize that their exchange partners are also—to a degree—*dependent* on rewards. Older partners must learn, in effect, the importance of negotiating from strength (Komorita, 1977), and they must recognize that they do have the power and ability to influence exchange outcomes. Consequently, if an old person perceives that an unbalanced exchange is becoming less profitable (either costs increase, or rewards decrease, or both), he or she may *change* the situation by *withholding* rewards anticipated by the other person. This strategy carries with it the risk of dissolving the relationship, but, in most cases, this risk is very small. A more likely outcome would be an increase in the rewards provided by the younger partner; in order to obtain whatever resource is controlled by the older parent, the middle-aged child will be required to *offer* more. In other words, by withholding a resource, the older person may change the exchange rate.

Perhaps the single greatest power resource possessed by the aged is their control over their Last Will and Testament. The ability of old people to "control" or exercise power in their relations with children and others is, in part, related to their control over the disposal of their estate; apparently, "even very small amounts of wealth and property" (Streib, 1976) are sufficient to constitute leverage. The old person can control this particular power resource by keeping all possible heirs uncertain as to their status in the will. As Streib points out, many old people are very adept in employing this resource and maximizing its utility by keeping their children "guessing about the provisions" (Streib, 1976, p. 166).

I should point out, however, that the utility of the last will by no means replaces or serves in lieu of the more generic types of power resources mentioned earlier. Although the normal use of the will is, as Sussman notes, simply an exchange of future blessings for current nurturance, there are several problems with the will as a resource. First of all, although the *existence* of a will may help an aged parent win considerable deference from children and other heirs, explicit *conversation* about the will is generally considered unfair usage. That is to say, in a specific negotiation with a possible heir, most old people are reluctant to use the will as an explicit voiced threat: "If you don't be nicer to me, I'll kick you out of the will." This approach seems *gauche* to many people, and, indeed, if the aged parent decides to change the relationship by using the will either explicitly or unethically, he or she runs the risk of losing the reward of contact maintenance with the child! But even for the less timid (or sensitive) individual who is willing to use a will as an explicit power resource and risk forfeiting a relationship, there is the additional risk of overusing the threat and thereby reducing its effectiveness. If the parent threatens too often to cut the child out of the will, then the child will probably slough off additional threats as merely the ramblings of an angry parent. However, in order to match the children's exchange resources, the aged parent may, in some cases, *have* to use the will explicitly and unethically.

A second problem related to using the Last Will and Testament as a power resource concerns the norms for determining appropriate shares in the will. Something similar to a "rule of distributive justice" seems to operate in the specific allocations of a last will. Sussman notes at least two rules concerning the will that most aged parents and adult children accept: first of all, according to Sussman (1976), "children feel that they should maintain intimate contact with aged parents . . . and that such contact maintenance is requisite for obtaining a share of inheritance"; secondly, the rule of distributive justice posits (and people generally accept) "the notion that the sibling who has rendered the greatest amount of service to an aged parent should receive a major portion of the inheritance upon the death of that parent" (p. 233).

The subject of power resources in general is an intriguing area of research because of the many possible "possessions" that people define as resources. Leggett (1972), for example, notes that old people "earn prestige partially on the basis of the class and racial content of the community." When a town comprises mostly white-collar and skilled workers, it acquires medium to high prestige. Its residents, according to Leggett, "identify with the area and acquire honor themselves, especially when they compare themselves invidiously with those living in communities with less honor" (p. 123). "Town honor" would probably constitute more of a resource in the interaction among old people than in cross-generational interaction (unless, of course, the younger person lives in a neighborhood with less prestige).

Another tactic that people use to maximize whatever power resources they have—one that applies to large groups of old people in their relations with other age groups qua political interest groups—is the mobilization of an age-based social movement. This form of collective behavior requires, in order to be effective, strong leadership and an effective organizational structure. Other conditions, such as the structural prerequisites identified by Smelser (1963), must also be present, however, before an old-age social movement can be postulated with any certainty. A more effective first step than the development of a social movement (which is unlikely for old people in the 1980s) toward maximizing power resources would be the development of a sense of political efficacy and age conciousness. An age-based class consciousness is not only possible, but likely, given the numbers of people aged 65 and over by the year 2020 and the prospects of a slow-growth or "managed" economy in the years ahead. As in all social movements, participation entails a loss of individual power (time and resources spent in achieving movement objectives) but promises at the same time "the greater power of combined resources" (Coleman, 1973).[4]

[4]The issue of an age-based social movement is too broad and, perhaps, too remote to permit an extensive discussion here. For the interested reader, the following sources are recommended: Abu-Laban and Abu-Laban (1977); Barron (1961); Estes (1977); Ragan and Dowd (1974); Streib (1965); and Ward (1977).

Although some writers view the last twenty years as a period of tremendous progress for the aged, it is still too early for optimism concerning the future of the aged in American society. Status gaps between the old and the non-old remain large, and existing evidence suggests that they will remain at least as large in the foreseeable future. In exchange terms, this suggests that the power of old people to influence exchange rates will continue to be minimal. Of course, this may change, given the possibility of future old-age cohorts that may possess considerably higher levels of power resources (greater education, for example) than previous old-age cohorts. One should not be misled, however, to make optimistic conclusions about the status of old people just because existing data shows some improvement over the last few decades in the life situations of the population over 65. In making such conclusions one is really comparing quite different populations; a person aged 65 in 1940 was "older" then than a person aged 65 today. In contemporary American society, the entry into old age for most people—judged in terms of physical functioning and activity levels—is not at age 65 but much later. Consequently, to address the issues relating to *old* age one must recognize that the age group in question consists of people in their seventies and older.

Although I am usually optimistic, I have great difficulty agreeing with those who root their optimism about the future of the aged in existing structural arrangements. Cameron (1974, p. 153), for example, argues that "the tremendous strides made by the elderly . . . their political visibility and power, have developed largely as a result of the activities of their special interest groups." She also notes that, "largely through the two White House Conferences on Aging," there has been "a renewed respect for the last stage of the life cycle." The accuracy of both statements, in my view, is dubious. Although old-age interest groups did have some impact on the 1971 White House Conference, the Conference itself had no meaningful impact and so, I would argue, dashed any hopes that were raised during conference preparation.

One wonders, however, whether the *bargaining position* of old people could be significantly improved. The answer is a qualified "yes." The status of old people *can* be improved, but it will require a modification of existing behaviors that may not be possible. The key to all of this is *engagement*. In order for old people to improve their negotiating positions vis-à-vis younger partners they must remain engaged in exchange networks. This is because exchange relations tend toward balance; however, in order for the balanced state to evolve, the exchange relationship must endure. Consequently, even though a strategy of negotiation by default may be a rational response to an unbalanced exchange *in the short run*, the long-term solution requires old people to remain active and engaged. The withdrawal into private life, which is characteristic not only of old people but of many in the working class as well, runs counter to the best interests of these groups. Older people must strive to resist the "interiority" that presumably accompanies the entry into old age. The aged must join other outcasts and outsiders—"the exploited and persecuted of other races and colors, the unemployed and the unemployable" —who exist outside the democratic process (Marcuse, 1964, p. 265).

Engagement and activity may be difficult achievements for old people. *Increased* costs are the major reason why many people choose to disengage in old age; if they remain *active* exchange partners, they certainly will accrue even *greater* costs. Engagement is, however, the only means by which old-age status will improve. Old people must engage themselves in the course of their everyday social interactions. They must begin to appreciate the substantial degree of power they do possess.

This strategy is made more difficult to follow by the fact that age-segregated environments seem to produce considerably more primary-group ties among old people than settings in which there are actors of all ages. Hochschild's (1973) study of the occupants of Merrill Court and Rosow's (1967) earlier research on social integration each arrive at this conclusion. The reason for this is relatively straightforward. In our age-stratified society, old age is devalued and so, too, as a consequence, are old people. In cross-age social exchanges, then, age becomes a pivotal status characteristic, the criterion used to determine the going rates of exchange. Old people invariably are disadvantaged in such relationships. In settings comprised solely of old people, however, age stratification is largely eliminated. (I say "largely" eliminated because there is still the possibility that invidious distinctions may emerge between younger and older groups of old people). The status differences that do emerge are based more on "achieved" criteria. Personality characteristics and other personal resources become the bases underlying the distribution of prestige. Ross (1977) observed this to be true in her study of a French retirement complex: "Common in communities of older people is a shared understanding that material differences, with their origin in the past, are to be muted. New signals of status distinction are just as often part of these emerging shared understandings" (p. 181).

Given the higher probability of primary-group relationships among age peers in an age-homogeneous environment, it is with serious reservations that I recommend the continued engagement of old people in cross-age exchange networks. The alternative course of social withdrawal (or restriction of interactions, to the maximum extent feasible, to those with age peers) does nothing to change the underlying problem. The status of old people will *not* improve through reliance upon the good will of younger people or the good intentions of concerned organizations. Such interventions may alleviate certain conditions but, by not addressing the central issue of power and dependence, they offer no real solution.

Present policies can assist old people to remain engaged in society by providing whatever benefits they are entitled to *directly to* the old people themselves; that is, wherever possible, rather than develop services *for* old people, these people should be allowed the freedom to decide whether this service or a similar service provided by a different supplier (or even a completely different product or service) will be purchased. In addition to actively engaging old people in society, this would have the benefit of increasing the likelihood that the services will be used to enlarge the older person's exchange networks and enhance his or her position within existing relationships. As Suttles and Street (1970, p. 753) note, "in this way, each recipient could become a benefactor within his own horizon or strata."[5]

The central issue in resolving the problems of the aged, as we discussed earlier, is individual autonomy. Our social policies must reflect a respect for individual freedom. This respect requires that we consider old people in all their diversity and resist categorizing old people according to the stereotypes of "sick," "useless," or "senile." Perhaps the single most damaging conception of old age is that old age is a period of life without significant *potential*. We tend to perceive old people as a group without a future, without the potential for continued growth and change. Old age is viewed as a period in which time stops. People cease to look to the future; they stop anticipating and planning for future events. Old age is, in a word, superfluous.[6]

This conception, irrespective of any prior validity it might have had, no longer fairly characterizes old age. Old people have a tremendous potential for societal contribution and self-growth that is currently not being exercised. Our stereotypes about old age, which are learned and internalized by old people themselves, violate the principle of respect for the individual person. To the extent that each of us tends to perceive old age in the same fashion, we become part of the problem. Since we are all growing old, we all have a vested interest in improving the status of old people. The necessary first step is the development of an appreciation of individual differences among old people. In concordance with the principle of respect, we must, as Lukes cogently argues:

> regard and act toward individuals in their concrete specificity, that we take full account of their (social) situations. . . . this means in practice, among other things, that we see them as the (actually or potentially) autonomous sources of decisions and choices, as engaging in activities and involvements that they value highly and that require protection from public interference, and as capable of realizing certain potentialities, which will take a distinctive form in each specific individual's case. . . . it requires us to see each of them as an actually or potentially autonomous centre of choice . . . able to choose be-

---

[5] Sussman's proposal that old people be provided cash sums that could be used to contract services from their adult children is consistent with this principle.

[6] Mizruchi makes a similar point in his analysis of time and aging (1977).

tween, and on occasion transcend, socially given activities and involvements, and to develop his or her respective potentialities [1973, pp. 148–149].

Although I recognize that most of us will continue to interact with old people in stereotypical fashion, I also believe that the inequality among age groups in our society will persist as long as we continue to discount the importance of autonomy in daily life. The status of the aged (and our *perceptions* of old people) is undeniably rooted in the nature of modern, post-industrial society. It would be a mistake, however, to argue that a change in political economy is, then, the only means by which the relative status of old people can be improved. Remembering that social structure exists ultimately in the countless social interactions of individuals, one can see how structural arrangements can indeed be modified as a result of changes in the interactions among social actors.

Since each of us, as an individual, is powerless to affect directly the nature of our political economy, we must use social interaction as an indirect —but the most viable—avenue of approach. Age status will change if social actors no longer accept age as a legitimate reason for determining shares of privilege in society. Although the elimination of age as a relevant status characteristic in the negotiation of exchange rates may work against the short-term interests of the younger exchange partner, we all stand to benefit in the long run. Since each of us will, in time, become old, the conduct of social exchange that is "blind" to age is in the best interests of us all.

Review Questions

1. Discuss the relationship between individualism and community.
2. What is the "paternalistic assertion"?
3. How is the strategy of "negotiation by default" used by old people to rebalance their exchange relations?
4. The central fact of life in old age is the struggle to remain independent. Discuss.
5. Although the Last Will may be an important power resource for old people, what are some of the difficulties they could encounter in using this resource in social exchange?

Glossary

activity theory: a theory stressing the importance for the individual of continuing patterns of activity or involvement into later life.

aging effect: a change between two measuring points in some aspect of an individual or group that is due to maturation, particularly biological maturation.

agrarian society: a society in which members subsist on what they produce from the land, thus requiring a large, cheap labor force.

armored-defensive personality: a type of person who attempts to defend herself or himself from perceived threats associated with aging by erecting defenses against anxiety through social disengagement.

boundaries: demarcation lines between discrete social units like age strata; points or zones where social interaction begins or ends.

bourgeoisie: owners of the productive resources.

bureaucracy: an organization with an extensive hierarchy and division of labor governed by explicit rules.

bureaucratization: the process by which the major tasks and functions of society come to be performed increasingly by bureaucratic organizations.

capitalism: an economic system characterized by freedom of the market with increasing concentration of private and corporate ownership of production and distribution facilities, proportionate to increasing accumulation and reinvestment of profits. Marx saw it as a system that is based on the exploitation of the proletariat.

charisma: a rare quality or power attributed to those who have demonstrated extraordinary success in social interaction; often thought to be divinely inspired.

class consciousness: awareness of membership in a class with its associated inequalities and political role.

cohort: all individuals born in the same year (or set of years); all individuals who enter a particular system or organization at the same time (for example, an incoming cohort of graduate students at a particular university).

cohort effect: a difference between individuals (or groups of individuals) of different ages that is due to their membership in different cohorts. The difference may be due to the unique matrix of experience of a particular cohort or to the structural composition (for example, size) of the cohort.

collective conscience: in Durkheim's view, the sum total of beliefs and sentiments common to the average of the members of society that persists over time and so serves to unite the generations.

conflict theory: a sociological theory that argues that social life involves interest groups in conflict over who shall have power and that social systems tend to change as a result of this conflict.

decision rule: a group of norms, including rationality and distributive justice, that are used as the basis of negotiating and conducting social exchange.

deference: the ritual or ceremonial dramatizing of an individual's or group's priority.

deindividuation: a condition of relative anonymity in which group members do not feel singled out or identifiable.

dependence: the inability to reciprocate a rewarding behavior; the degree to which actors are unable to do without the service or resource provided by another.

disengagement theory: a theory emphasizing an inevitable mutual withdrawal that occurs gradually between the aging person and others.

distributive justice: a concept developed by Homans that states that interaction between two social actors is equitable when the ratio of one person's profits (rewards minus costs) to investments is the same as the second person's ratio.

dual-economy theory (dual-labor-market theory): a theory of stratification that argues that the industrial structure is divisible into distinct sectors (usually *core* and *periphery* sectors) within which workers face fundamentally different conditions. Industries in the periphery sector may be differentiated from those in the core in that they are usually smaller, non-unionized, oriented toward service rather than production, and operate in a relatively open, competitive capitalistic environment.

embourgeoisiement: the idea that, with increases in education and income, the working-class member is becoming less working class and more middle class.

eschaton: a vision of the future in apocalyptic terms; a belief that tomorrow will bring an abrupt, quite likely violent but assuredly total, disruption to the world order as we have known it.

exchange theory: a view of social behavior as consisting of the voluntary actions of individuals that are motivated by the returns they are expected to bring, and typically do bring, from others. Recent developments in exchange theory have emphasized the importance of power in the conduct of social exchange.

extended family: a household consisting of married couples from different generations, their children, and other relatives.

false consciousness: in Marxist theory, the idea that the proletariat may not feel alienated or recognize its alienation.

functional theory of stratification: a theory generated by structural functionalists that says that the differential rewards of a stratification system are necessary to motivate the most able people to take on the most important tasks of the society.

gemeinschaft: a type of society or community in which people are valued for their personal qualities rather than material wealth and people's relationships are based on intimacy and tradition.

generation: the position of a person such as child, parent, or grandparent in the ranked descent within a family; offspring having a common parent or parents and constituting a single stage of descent.

gesellschaft: a society characterized by impersonal and limited relationships, such as modern industrial societies.

human capital: a view of the labor market as being composed of rational workers who invest in training that will maximize their economic return (income) on investments; the individual's personal resources such as education, IQ, or job training that can be used to maximize his or her position in the marketplace.

hunting and gathering societies: societies with simple economies where food was obtained by hunting wild game and gathering wild fruits and plants. In Lenski's evolutionary theory, hunting and gathering societies occurred until about 7000 B.C.

ideology: a system of ideas and beliefs about the world or some aspect of it; a system of beliefs held by a group that reflects, rationalizes, and defends the group's own interests, justifying that group's behavior, goals, attitudes, and values.

Industrial Revolution: the change in economic life that occurred between 1760 and 1830 and that involved the substitution of machines for hand tools and inanimate sources of energy for human and animal power.

industrial society: a society in which a substantial proportion of the labor force is involved in the production of goods.

interiority: increased awareness of and emphasis on one's own experience and inner thought processes; believed to accompany old age and to be associated with a decline in sensitivity to events in the immediate environment.

interpretive sociology: an approach to sociology that emphasizes the importance of subjective interpretation or meaning attached to social phenomena.

"Iron Cage": Weber's image of the development of the world in which individuality and creativity would disappear in the face of the inexorable advance of bureaucratization and rationalization.

legitimate: to provide support or justification for an existing social order.

life cycle: the distinctive periods of a person's life: infancy, childhood, adolescence, adulthood, old age.

macro-level analysis: sociological research that focuses on large-scale social systems (such as formal organizations or cities) and patterns of interrelationships within and between these systems.

micro-level analysis: sociological research that focuses on individuals or the social interaction of individuals as the unit of analysis.

modernization theory: an evolutionary view that argues that traditional (pre-industrial) societies change their basic structure through economic development and industrialization in order to survive. This change occurs through such processes as structural differentiation and proceeds through various stages that produce a more complex and mobile society ready to deal with industrial technology.

monopolistic capitalism: a stage in the development of capitalism in which a few large organizations in each industry dominate and "peacefully coexist," instead of being involved in open competition.

neolocal residence: a type of family-residence pattern in which a newly married couple lives apart from both the husband's and wife's relatives.

norm: an expectation widely shared within society (or a subgroup of society); standards for behavior that members of a group share, to which they are expected to conform, and that are enforced by positive and negative sanctions.

normative sociology: a view of socialization as a mechanism of effecting conformity to shared expectations about values and behavior; a view of the self as being constituted by internalized social norms.

normlessness: a situation characterized by a lack of clear-cut guidelines and rules controlling and dictating "proper" conduct.

Oedipus complex: a process in psychoanalytic theory that occurs in the phallic stage (age 3–5 years). The male child becomes sexually attracted to his mother and jealous of his father. The complex is resolved by the child's identification with the father and transformation of desire for the mother into gentle affection.

off-time: entering some role or activity at a point in the life course generally considered too early or too late to be optimal or appropriate.

operational definition: the actual questions or techniques used to measure the concept or idea being studied.

patrilineal: a cultural pattern tracing descent through the father's group.

patrilocal residence: a type of family residence pattern in which a newly married couple lives with or near the husband's family.

period effect: a change between two measuring points in some aspect of an individual or group that is due to sociohistorical events (or cultural shifts) occurring in the interval between measurements.

post-industrial society: a society in which the percentage of those employed in agriculture stabilizes at a very low level, with a continuing decrease of the percentage in manufacturing and increase of the percentage in service-related industries.

power: a situation where one actor is less dependent on services or resources held by others than the others are on services or resources held by the actor; the ability to reciprocate a rewarding behavior and thereby, maintain a balanced or favorable exchange rate.

power resource: a commodity or service exchanged in social interaction that allows the person to maintain balanced exchange relationships; that which an actor possesses that enables the actor to negotiate a favorable exchange rate.

pre-industrial society: a society in which the vast majority of the population is engaged in agriculture.

privilege: the possession or control of a portion of the surplus produced by the members of a society.

proletariat: workers employed by the owners; the subordinate class in capitalist societies composed of those who do not own the means of production and who must sell their labor in order to survive.

qualitative methodology: an approach to research that uses descriptive accounts, presenting data in detailed words (parts of conversations, for example) rather than in numerical fashion.

quantitative methodology: an approach to research that uses numerical measurement, presenting data in numbers rather than in words.

reciprocity: a "give-and-take" process in social interaction whereby a person who gives something of value to another expects to receive something back of approximately equal value.

rocking-chair personality: a type of person who voluntarily and contentedly withdraws from responsibilities and involvements in old age.

role: a system of norms and values that provides the script (rules for behavior) for an incumbent of a given status.

role strain: personal distress resulting from too many role expectations.

role theory: an orientation to the study of social behavior that emphasizes the importance of roles and norms in shaping behavior.

Rustum complex: the desire of a father to kill his son; grounded in the Persian myth concerning the death of Sohrab by his father Rustum.

social class: a social group whose members have a similar relation to the means of production and who, at some point, develop class consciousness.

social gerontology: a subfield of gerontology dealing with (1) the attitudes and behaviors of old people; (2) social interactions involving at least one old person; (3) the structural causes and consequences of having more or fewer old people in the population; and (4) the social problems old people face.

social interaction: action that mutually affects two or more individuals.

social movement: a large number of people acting with some rudimentary organization to seek more power or to maintain the power they have.

social structure: a relatively enduring system of norms, values, and social relationships; a pattern of interaction among people that has a discernible form and shape.

sociobiology: a new discipline that focuses on the biological basis for social behavior in species ranging from amoebas to human beings.

status: the position an individual or group occupies in society.

status attainment theory: a view that social mobility and the differential placement of individuals in the socioeconomic hierarchy is a reflection of the individual characteristics, such as IQ, education, or personal aspirations, brought into the marketplace by the worker.

status inconsistency: differences in an individual's (or group's) positions in several stratification hierarchies.

stratification: the ranking of groups of people according to characteristics such as power, with some higher (more prestige, power, property) and some lower.

stratum: an aggregate of persons who stand in a similar position with respect to force or some specific form of institutionalized power, privilege, or prestige; persons who stand in relation to each other by virtue of common interests (for example, age, money, gender).

structural functionalism: an approach to sociological theory that studies society as a set of relatively stable and patterned social units, and the adjustment of these parts to the whole; views society as being made up of interdependent parts, with norms guiding status roles, statuses being interconnected to form institutions, and institutions being interdependent in larger society.

symbolic interactionism: a sociological theory based on the view that our humanness derives from the mutual impact we have on one another. It depicts us as active agents who in the course of social interaction consciously, deliberately, and directly fashion our personal histories and the history of the world about us. It emphasizes the part that language and gestures play in the formation of mind, self, and society.

theory: a set of ideas, or concepts, that are useful in understanding and explaining a broad range of social phenomena.

References

Abercrombie, N., & Turner, B. S. The dominant ideology thesis. *British Journal of Sociology,* 1978, *29,* 149–170.

Abrahamson, M., Mizruchi, E. H., & Hornung, C. A. *Stratification and mobility.* New York: Macmillan, 1976.

Abrams, P. Rites de passage: The conflict of generations in industrial society. *Journal of Contemporary History,* 1970, *5,* 175–190.

Abramson, P. R. Generational change in American electoral behavior. *American Political Science Review,* 1974, *68,* 93–105.

Abramson, P. R. *Generational change in American politics.* Lexington, Mass.: D. C. Heath, 1975.

Abu-Laban, S. M., & Abu-Laban, B. Women and the aged as minority groups: A critique. *The Canadian Review of Sociology and Anthropology,* 1977, *14,* 103–116.

Achenbaum, W. A. The obsolescence of old age in America. *Journal of Social History,* 1974, *2,* 48–62.

Adams, B. N. The middle-class adult and his widowed or still-married mother. *Social Problems,* 1968, *16,* 50–59.

Adams, R. N. *Energy and structure.* Austin: University of Texas, 1975.

Agnello, T. J., Jr. Aging and the sense of political powerlessness. *Public Opinion Quarterly,* 1973, *37,* 251–259.

Albee, E. *The American dream.* New York: Coward-McCann, 1961.

Alberoni, F. Classes and generations. *Social Science Information,* 1971, *10,* 41–67.

Allen, M. P. The structure of interorganizational elite cooptation: Interlocking corporate directorates. *American Sociological Review,* 1974, *39,* 393–406.

Allen, S. Class, culture, and generation. *Sociological Review,* 1973, *21,* 437–446.

Anderson, B. G. The process of deculturation: Its dynamics among the United States aged. *Anthropological Quarterly,* 1972, *45,* 209–216.

Anderson, B. & Davis, N. J. Boundary crossings in social networks: A semiotic trial formulation. In D. Willer and B. Anderson (Eds.), *Social exchange and social networks.* New York: Elsevier, 1979.

Anderson, C. H. *The political economy of social classes.* Englewood Cliffs, N. J.: Prentice-Hall, 1974.

Archibald, W. P. Face-to-face: The alienating effects of class, status, and power differences. *American Sociological Review,* 1976, *41,* 819–837.

Arling, G., Parham, I. A., & Teitelman, J. *Learned helplessness and social exchange: Convergence and application of theories.* Paper presented at the Annual Meetings of the Gerontological Society, Dallas, 1978.

Atchley, R. C. The life course, age grading, and age-linked demands for decision making. In N.

Datan and L. Ginsburg (Eds.), *Life-span developmental psychology: Normative life crises.* New York: Academic Press, 1975.

Atchley, R. C. *The sociology of retirement.* Cambridge, Mass.: Schenkman, 1976.

Averitt, R. T. *The dual economy: The dynamics of American industry structure.* New York: Horton, 1968.

Back, K. W. Personal characteristics and social behavior: Theory and method. In R. Binstock and E. Shanas (Eds.), *Handbook of aging and the social sciences.* New York: Van Nostrand Reinhold, 1976.

Balswick, J. The Jesus people movement: A generational interpretation. *Journal of Social Issues,* 1974, *30,* 23–42.

Baltes, P. B., & Willis, S. L. Toward psychological theories of aging and development. In J. E. Birren and K. W. Schaie (Eds.), *Handbook of the psychology of aging.* New York: Van Nostrand Reinhold, 1977.

Baran, P., & Sweezy, P. *Monopoly capital: An essay in the American economic and social order.* New York: Monthly Review, 1966.

Baron, H. M. Racial domination in advanced capitalism: A theory of nationalism and divisions in the labor market. In R. Edwards, M. Reich, and D. Gordon (Eds.), *Labor market segmentation.* Lexington, Mass.: D. C. Heath, 1973.

Barron, M. L. *The aging American: An introduction to social gerontology and geriatrics.* New York: Thomas Y. Crowell, 1961.

Baum, R. C., & Baum, M. The aged and diachronic solidarity in modern society. *International Journal of Aging and Human Development,* 1975, *6,* 329–346.

Beck, E. M., Horan, P. M., & Tolbert, C. M., III. Stratification in a dual economy: A sectoral model of earnings determination. *American Sociological Review,* 1978, *43,* 704–720.

Becker, G. S. *Human capital.* New York: National Bureau of Economic Research, 1964.

Becker, G. S. *The economics of discrimination.* Chicago: University of Chicago Press, 1971.

Becker, H. *Man in reciprocity.* New York: F. A. Praeger, 1956.

Bell, D. *The coming of post-industrial society.* New York: Basic Books, 1973.

Ben-David, J. The state of sociological theory and the sociological community. *Comparative Studies in Society and History,* 1973, *15,* 448–472.

Bengtson, V. L., & Black, K. D. Intergenerational relations and continuities in socialization. In P. B. Baltes and K. W. Schaie (Eds.), *Life-span developmental psychology: Personality and socialization.* New York: Academic Press, 1973.

Bengtson, V. L. & Cutler, N. E. Generations and intergenerational relations: Perspectives on time, age groups, and social change. In R. Binstock and E. Shanas (Eds.), *Handbook of aging and the social sciences.* New York: Van Nostrand Reinhold, 1976.

Bengtson, V. L., & Dowd, J. J. Functionalism, exchange, and life-cycle analysis. *International Journal of Aging and Human Development,* in press.

Bengtson, V. L., Dowd, J. J., Smith, D. H., & Inkeles, A. Modernization, modernity, and perceptions of aging: A cross-cultural survey. *Journal of Gerontology,* 1975, *30,* 688–695.

Bengtson, V. L., Furlong, M., & Laufer, R. Time, aging, and the continuity of social structure: Themes and issues in generational analysis. *Journal of Social Issues,* 1974, *30,* 1–30.

Berger, B. How long is a generation? *British Journal of Sociology,* 1960, *2,* 10–23.

Berger, J., & Fisek, M. H. Consistent and inconsistent status characteristics and the determination of power and prestige orders. *Sociometry,* 1970, *33,* 287–304.

Berger, J., Fisek, M. H., Norman, R. Z., & Zelditch, M., Jr. *Status characteristics and social interaction: An expectation-status approach.* New York: Elsevier, 1977.

Berger, P. L. *Facing up to modernity.* New York: Basic Books, 1975.

Berger, P. L., Berger, B., & Kellner, H. *The homeless mind: Modernization and consciousness.* New York: Random House, 1973.

Berger, P. L., & Luckmann, T. *The social construction of reality.* New York: Anchor Doubleday, 1966.

Bershady, H. J. On Davis and Moore again, or: Dissensus and the stability of social systems. *British Journal of Sociology,* 1970, *21,* 446–454.

Bettelheim, B. The problem of generations. *Daedalus,* 1962, *91,* 68–96.

Bierstedt, R. An analysis of social power. *American Sociological Review,* 1950, *15,* 730–738.

Binstock, R. H. Interest-group liberalism and the politics of aging. *Gerontologist,* 1972, *12,* 265–280.

Blau, P. M. *Exchange and power in social life.* New York: Wiley, 1964. (a)

Blau, P. M. Justice in social exchange. *Sociological Inquiry,* 1964, *34,* 193–206. (b)

Blau, P. M. Parameters of social structure. *American Sociological Review,* 1974, *39,* 615–635.

Blau, P. M. *Inequality and heterogeneity: A primative theory of social structure.* New York: Free Press, 1977.

Blenkner, M. Social work and family relationships in later life. In E. Shanas and G. Streib (Eds.), *Social structure and the family: Generational relations.* Englewood Cliffs, N. J.: Prentice-Hall, 1965.

Bluestone, B. The characteristics of marginal industries. In David M. Gorden (Ed.), *Problems in political economy.* Lexington, Mass.: D. C. Heath, 1977.

Bluestone, B., Murphy, W. M., & Stevenson, M. *Low wages and the working poor.* Ann Arbor: Institute of Labor and Industrial Relations, University of Michigan, 1973.

Bonacich, E. Abolition, the extension of slavery, and the position of free Blacks: A study of split labor markets in the United States, 1830–1863. *American Journal of Sociology,* 1975, *81,* 601–628.

Bonacich, E. Advanced capitalism and Black/White relations in the United States: A split labor market interpretation. *American Sociological Review,* 1976, *41,* 34–51.

Bottomore, T. B. *Classes in modern society.* New York: Vintage, 1968.

Bottomore, T. B., & Ruber, M. (Eds.). *Karl Marx: Selected writings in sociology and social philosophy.* New York: McGraw-Hill, 1964. (T. B. Bottomore, trans.)

Bowles, S. Schooling and inequality from generation to generation. *Journal of Political Economy,* 1972, *80,* 219–251.

Brittan, A. *The privatised world.* London: Routledge & Kegan Paul, 1977.

Britton, J. H., Mather, W. G., & Lansing, A. K. Expectations for older persons in a rural community: Living arrangements and family relationships. *Journal of Gerontology,* 1961, *16,* 156–162.

Browder, D. R. Fathers, sons, and grandfathers: Social origins of radical intellectuals in nineteenth-century Russia. *Journal of Social History,* 1969, *2,* 333–355.

Buckley, W. On equitable inequality. *American Sociological Review,* 1963, *28,* 799–801.

Burgess, E. W. Aging in western culture. In E. W. Burgess (Ed.), *Aging in Western societies.* Chicago: University of Chicago Press, 1960.

Cain, G. G. The challenge of segmented labor-market theories to orthodox theory. *Journal of Economic Literature,* 1976, *14,* 1215–1257.

Cain, L. D. Life course and social structure. In R. E. L. Faris (Ed.), *Handbook of sociology.* Chicago: Rand McNally, 1964.

Cain, L. D. Age status and generational phenomena: The new old people in contemporary America. *Gerontologist,* 1967, *7,* 83–92.

Cain, L. D. The growing importance of legal age in determining the status of the elderly. *The Gerontologist,* 1974, *14,* 167–174.

Cain, L. D. Aging and the law. In R. Binstock and E. Shanas (Eds.), *Handbook of aging and the social sciences.* New York: Van Nostrand Reinhold, 1976.

Cameron, S. W. The politics of the elderly. *The Midwest Quarterly,* 1974, *15,* 141–153.

Carchedi, G. *On the economic identification of social classes.* London: Routledge & Kegan Paul, 1977.

Carlsson, G., & Karlsson, K. Age, cohorts, and the generation of generations. *American Sociological Review,* 1970, *35,* 710–717.

Cavan, R. S., Burgess, E. W., Havighurst, R., & Goldhammer, H. *Personal adjustment in old age.* Chicago: Science Research Associates, 1949.

Christoffersen, T. Gerontology: Towards a general theory and a research strategy. *Acta Sociologica,* 1974, *17,* 393–407.

Clark, M. Patterns of aging among the elderly poor of the inner city. *Gerontologist,* 1971, *11,* 58–66.

Clausen, J. A. The life course of individuals. In M. Riley, M. Johnson, and A. Foner (Eds.), *Aging and society,* Volume III of *A Sociology of Age Stratification.* New York: Russell Sage, 1972.

Cohen, C., & Sokolovsky, J. *Sociability of SRO aged—a reassessment.* Paper presented at the Annual Meetings of the Gerontological Society, Dallas, 1978.

Coleman, J. S. Loss of power. *American Sociological Review,* 1973, *38,* 1–17.

Collins, R. *Conflict sociology: Toward an explanatory science.* New York: Academic Press, 1975.

Cook, K. S. Exchange and power in networks of interorganizational relations. *The Sociological Quarterly*, 1977, *18*, 62–82.

Cooley, C. H. *Social organization*. New York: Scribners, 1912.

Cottrell, L. S., Jr. The life adjustment of the individual to his age and sex roles. *American Sociological Review*, 1942, *7*, 617–620.

Cowgill, D. O. The aging of populations and societies. *Annals of the American Academy of Political and Social Science*, 1974, *415*, 1–18. (a)

Cowgill, D. O. Aging and modernization: A revision of the theory. In J. F. Gubrium (Ed.), *Late life: Communities and environmental policy*. Springfield, Ill.: Charles C Thomas, 1974. (b)

Cowgill, D. O., & Holmes, L. D. *Aging and modernization*. New York: Appleton-Century-Crofts, 1972.

Creighton, M. *A case for mandatory retirement*. Paper presented at the Annual Meetings of the Pacific Sociological Association, Spokane, Washington, 1978.

Crittenden, J. Aging and party affiliation. *Public Opinion Quarterly*, 1962, *26*, 648–657.

Crittenden, J. Aging and political participation. *Western Political Quarterly*, 1963, *16*, 323–331.

Crompton, R., & Gubbay, J. *Economy and class structure*. New York: St. Martin's Press, 1978.

Cumming, E., & Henry, W. *Growing old: The process of disengagement*. New York: Basic Books, 1961.

Curtin, S. *Nobody ever died of old age*. Boston: Little, Brown, 1972.

Cutler, N. E. Generation, maturation, and party affiliation: A cohort analysis. *Public Opinion Quarterly*, 1969, *33*, 583–588.

Cutler, N. E., & Bengtson, V. L. Age and political alienation: Maturation, generation, and period effects. *Annals of the American Academy of Political and Social Science*, 1974, *415*, 160–175.

Cutler, S., & Kaufman, R. L. Cohort changes in political attitudes: Tolerance of ideological nonconformity. *Public Opinion Quarterly*, 1975, *39*, 69–81.

Dahrendorf, R. *Class and class conflict in industrial society*. Stanford: Stanford University Press, 1959.

Dalton, R. J. Was there a revolution? A note on generational versus life cycle explanations of value differences. *Comparative Political Studies*, 1977, *9*, 459–473.

Davis, K. The abominable heresy: A reply to Dr. Buckley. *American Sociological Review*, 1959, *24*, 82–83.

Davis, K., & Moore, W. E. Some principles of stratification. *American Sociological Review*, 1945, *10*, 242–249.

Davis, M. S., & Schmidt, C. J. The obnoxious and the nice. *Sociometry*, 1977, *40*, 201–213.

Dawe, A. The two sociologies. *British Journal of Sociology*, 1970, *21*, 207–218.

Dawkins, R. *The selfish gene*. New York: Oxford University Press, 1976

de Beauvoir, S. *The coming of age* (P. O'Brian, trans.). New York: Putnam's, 1972.

Domhoff, G. W. *The bohemian grove and other retreats: A study of ruling-class cohesiveness*. New York: Harper & Row, 1974.

Domhoff, G. W. Social clubs, policy-planning groups, and corporations: A network study of ruling-class cohesiveness. *Insurgent Sociologist*, 1975, *5*, 173–184.

Dooley, P. C. The interlocking directorate. *American Economic Review*, 1969, *59*, 314–323.

Douglass, E. B., Cleveland, W. P., & Maddox, G. L. Political attitudes, age, and aging: A cohort analysis of archival data. *Journal of Gerontology*, 1974, *29*, 666–675.

Dowd, J. J. Aging as exchange: A preface to theory. *Journal of Gerontology*, 1975, *30*, 584–594. (a)

Dowd, J. J. Distributive justice and psychological reactance. *Pacific Sociological Review*, 1975, *18*, 421–441. (b)

Dowd, J. J. Aging and the American dream. Unpublished manuscript, 1978. (a)

Dowd, J. J. Aging as exchange: A test of the distributive justice proposition. *Pacific Sociological Review*, 1978, *21*, 351–375. (b)

Dowd, J. J., & Brooks, F. P., III. *Age and anomia: Normlessness or class consciousness?* Paper presented at the Annual Meetings of the Gerontological Society, Dallas, 1978.

Dowd, J. J., & LaRossa, R. *Primary group contact and elderly morale*. Paper presented at the Annual Meetings of the Gerontological Society, Dallas, 1978.

Duberman, L. *Social inequality: Class and caste in America*. Philadelphia: J. B. Lippincott, 1976.

Durkheim, E. *The Division of Labor in Society* (G. Simpson, trans.). Glencoe, Ill.: Free Press, 1947.

Eisenstadt, S. N. *From generation to generation: Age groups and social structure.* New York: Free Press, 1971. (Originally published in 1956.)

Elder, G. H., Jr. Age differentiation and the life course. In A. Inkeles, J. Coleman, and N. Smelser (Eds.), *Annual review of sociology* (Vol. 1). Palo Alto, Calif.: Annual Reviews, 1975.

Emerson, R. M. Power-dependence relations. *American Sociological Review,* 1962, *27,* 31–41.

Emerson, R. M. Exchange theory, parts 1 and 2. In J. Berger, M. Zelditch, and B. Anderson (Eds.), *Sociological theories in progress.* (Vol. 2). Boston: Houghton-Mifflin, 1972.

Emerson, R. M. Social exchange theory. In A. Inkeles, J. Coleman, and N. Smelser (Eds.), *Annual review of sociology* (Vol. 2). Palo Alto, Calif.: Annual Reviews, 1976.

Eros, J. The positivist generation of French Republicanism. *Sociological Review,* 1955, *3,* 255–277.

Esler, A. *Bombs, beards, and barricades: 150 years of youth in revolt.* New York: Stein & Day, 1971.

Estes, C. L. *Toward a sociology of political gerontology.* Paper presented at the Annual Meetings of the Western Gerontological Society, Denver, March, 1977.

Fairchild, T. J., Pruchno, R., & Kahana, E. *Implications of the social exchange theory for understanding the effect of reciprocity among the aged.* Paper presented at the Annual Meetings of the Gerontological Society, Dallas, 1978.

Featherman, D. L. Achievement orientations and socioeconomic career attainments. *American Sociological Review,* 1972, *37,* 131–143.

Feinman, S. Biosociological approaches to social behavior. In S. G. McNall (Ed.), *Theoretical perspectives in sociology.* New York: St. Martin's Press, 1979.

Feuer, L. S. *The conflict of generations.* New York: Basic Books, 1969.

Fischer, C. S., Jackson, R., Stueve, C., Gerson, K., Jones, L., & Baldassare, M. *Networks and places: Social relations in the urban setting.* New York: Free Press, 1977.

Fischer, D. H. *Growing old in America.* New York: Oxford, 1977.

Fisher, B. M., & Strauss, A. L. Interactionism. In T. Bottomore and R. Nisbet (Eds.), *A history of sociological analysis.* New York: Basic Books, 1978.

Foner, A. Age stratification and age conflict in political life. *American Sociological Review,* 1974, *39,* 187–196.

Foner, A. Age in society: Structure and change. *American Behavioral Scientist,* 1975, *19,* 144–165.

Foner, A. Age stratification and the changing family. In J. Demos and S. S. Boocock (Eds.), *Turning points: Historical and sociological essays on the family.* Chicago: University of Chicago Press, 1978.

Foner, A., & Kertzer, D. Transitions over the life course: Lessons from age-set societies. *American Journal of Sociology,* 1978, *83,* 1081–1104.

Frankfather, D. *The aged in the community: Managing senility and deviance.* New York: Praeger, 1977.

Freitag, P. J. The cabinet and big business: A study of interlocks. *Social Problems,* 1975, *23,* 137–152.

Gamson, W. A. *Power and discontent.* Homewood, Ill.: Dorsey, 1968.

Ganschow, T. W. The aged in a revolutionary milieu: China. In S. Spicker, K. Woodward, and D. D. van Tassel (Eds.), *Aging and the elderly.* Atlantic Highlands, N. J.: Humanities Press, 1978.

Giddens, A. *The class structure of the advanced societies.* London: Hutchinson & Co., 1973.

Gieryn, T. F. *Generation differences in the research interests of scientists.* Paper presented at the Annual Meetings of the American Sociological Association, Chicago, 1977.

Gilford, R. *Intergenerational predictivity of marital satisfaction: A covariance analysis.* Paper presented at the 11th International Congress of Gerontology, Tokyo, 1978.

Gilford, R., & Bengtson, V. L. *Correlates of marital satisfaction in old age.* Paper presented at the Annual Meetings of the Gerontological Society, San Francisco, 1977.

Glascock, A. P., & Feinman, S. L. A cross-cultural analysis of the determinants of old age. Paper presented at the Annual Meetings of the American Anthropological Association, Los Angeles, 1978.

Glenn, N. Cohort analysts' futile quest: Statistical attempts to separate age, period, and cohort effects. *American Sociological Review*, 1976, *41*, 900–904.

Goffman, E. *The presentation of self in everyday life*. Garden City, N. Y.: Doubleday Anchor, 1959.

Goode, W. J. The place of force in human society. *American Sociological Review*, 1972, *37*, 507–519.

Goody, J. Aging in nonindustrial societies. In R. Binstock and E. Shanas (Eds.), *Handbook of aging and the social sciences*. New York: Van Nostrand Reinhold, 1976.

Gouldner, A. W. *The coming crisis of Western sociology*. New York: Avon, 1970.

Gouldner, A. W. The sociologist as partisan: Sociology and the welfare state. In A. W. Gouldner (Ed.), *For sociology*. New York: Basic Books, 1973.

Greisman, H. C., & Ritzer, G. *Max Weber, critical theory, and the administered world*. Paper presented at the Annual Meetings of the American Sociological Association, San Francisco, 1978.

Griffiths, K. A., Farley, O. W., Dean, W. P., & Boon, L. L. Socio-economic class and the disadvantaged senior citizen. *International Journal of Aging and Human Development*, 1971, *2*, 288–296.

Gubrium, J. F. *The myth of the golden years: A socioenvironmental theory of aging*. Springfield, Ill.: Charles C. Thomas, 1973.

Gubrium, J. F. Notes on the social organization of senility. *Urban Life*, 1978, *7*, 23–44.

Gubrium, J. F., & Buckholdt, D. R. *Toward maturity*. San Francisco: Jossey-Bass, 1977.

Gusfield, J. R. The problem of generations in an organizational structure. *Social Forces*, 1957, *35*, 323–330.

Hajda, J. *Conflict and exchange theory: Two theories or one?* Paper presented at the Annual Meetings of the Pacific Sociological Association, Sacramento, 1977.

Halberstam, D. *The powers that be*. New York: Knopf, 1979.

Halebsky, S. *Mass society and political conflict*. Cambridge: Cambridge University Press, 1976.

Hall, P. M., & Hewitt, J. The quasi-theory of communication and the management of dissent. *Social Problems*, 1970, *18*, 17–27.

Halper, T. Paternalism and the elderly. In S. Spicker, K. Woodward, and D. van Tassel (Eds.), *Aging and the elderly*. Atlantic Highlands, N. J.: Humanities Press, 1978.

Harlan, W. H. Social status of the aged in three Indian villages. *Vita Humanae*, 1964, *7*, 239–252.

Hartung, J. On natural selection and the inheritance of wealth. *Current Anthropology*, 1976, *17*, 607–622.

Heilbroner, R. L. *An inquiry into the human prospect*. London: Calder & Boyars, 1975.

Hellman, S. Generational differences in the bureaucratic elite of Italian Communist party provincial federations. *Canadian Journal of Political Science/Revue Canadienne De Science Politique*, 1975, *8*, 82–106.

Henretta, J. C., & Campbell, R. T. Status attainment and status maintenance: A study of stratification in old age. *American Sociological Review*, 1976, *41*, 981–992.

Henretta, J. C., & Campbell, R. T. Net worth as an aspect of status. *American Journal of Sociology*, 1978, *83*, 1204–1223.

Hewitt, J. P., & Hall, P. M. Social problems, problematic situations, and quasi-theories. *American Sociological Review*, 1973, *38*, 367–374.

Hewitt, J. P., & Stokes, R. Disclaimers. *American Sociological Review*, 1975, *40*, 1–11.

Hochschild, A. R. *The unexpected community*. Englewood Cliffs, N. J.: Prentice-Hall, 1973.

Hogan, D. P. Order of events in the life course. *American Sociological Review*, 1978, *43*, 573–586.

Homans, G. C. *Social behavior: Its elementary forms*. New York: Harcourt, Brace & World, 1961.

Homans, G. C. *Sentiments and activities: Essays in social science*. New York: Free Press, 1962.

Homans, G. C. Bringing men back in. *American Sociological Review*, 1964, *29*, 809–818.

Homans, G. C. *Social behavior: Its elementary forms*. New York: Harcourt, Brace,& World, Jovanovich. 1974.

Horn, D. Youth resistance in the Third Reich: A social portrait. *Journal of Social History*, 1973, *7*, 26–50.

Horowitz, I. L. *Ideology and utopia in the United States, 1956–1976*. New York: Oxford University Press, 1977.

Hultsch, D. F., & Plemons, J. K. Life events and life-span development. In P. B. Baltes and O. G. Brim, Jr. (Eds.), *Life-span development and behavior* (Vol. 2). New York: Academic Press, 1979.

Huyck, M. H. *Psychosocial perspectives on adaptation in later life.* Paper presented at the 11th International Congress of Gerontology, Tokyo, 1978.

Inglehart, R. An end to European integrations? *American Political Science Review,* 1967, *61,* 91–105.

Inglehart, R. The silent revolution in Europe: Intergenerational change in industrial society. *American Political Science Review,* 1971, *65,* 991–1017.

Inkeles, A. A model of modern man: Theoretical and methodological issues. In N. Hammond (Ed.), *Social science and the new societies: Problems in cross-cultural research and theory building.* Lansing: Social Science Research Bureau, Michigan State University, 1973.

Jackson, E. F., & Curtis, R. F. Conceptualization and measurement in the study of social stratification. In H. Blalock and A. Blalock (Eds.), *Methodology in social research.* New York: McGraw-Hill, 1968.

Jacobs, D. Dependence and vulnerability: An exchange approach to the control of organizations. *Administrative Science Quarterly,* 1974, *19,* 45–59.

Jacobsen, S. G. *Dependency conditions among the elderly: Definition, assessment of factors, and implications for service.* Paper presented at the 11th International Congress of Gerontology, Tokyo, 1978.

Jaynes, J. *The origin of consciousness in the breakdown of the bicameral mind.* Boston: Houghton Mifflin, 1976.

Jennings, M. K., & Niemi, R. G. Continuity and change in political orientations: A longitudinal study of two generations. *American Political Science Review,* 1975, *69,* 1316–1335.

Johnson, G., & Kamara, J. L. Growing up and growing old: The politics of age exclusion. *International Journal of Aging and Human Development,* 1977, *8,* 99–110.

Jones, B. D. Path models of congressional voting: The case of the 1964 freshman democratic cohort. *Social Science Research,* 1974, *3,* 343–360.

Katz, S. H. Anthropological perspectives on aging. *Annals of the American Academy of Political and Social Sciences,* 1978, *438,* 1–12.

Kelley, H. H., & Thibaut, J. W. *Interpersonal relations: A theory of interdependence.* New York: Wiley, 1978.

Knoke, D., & Hout, M. Social and demographic factors in American political party affiliations. *American Sociological Review,* 1974, *39,* 700–713.

Komorita, S. S. Negotiating from strength and the concept of bargaining strength. *Journal for the Theory of Social Behavior,* 1977, *7,* 65–79.

Krauss, I. Some perspectives on social stratification and social class. *Sociological Review,* 1967, *15,* 129–140.

Krauss, I. *Stratification, class, and conflict.* New York: Free Press, 1976.

Kreisberg, L. Class conflicts. In M. Abrahamson, E. Mizruchi, and C. Hornung (Eds.), *Stratification and mobility.* New York: Macmillan, 1976.

Kreps, J. M. The economy and the aged. In R. Binstock and E. Shanas (Eds.), *Handbook of aging and the social sciences.* New York: Van Nostrand Reinhold, 1976.

Kuypers, J., & Bengtson, V. L. Social breakdown and competence: A social psychological view of aging. *Human Development,* 1973, *16,* 181–201.

Landtman, G. *The origin of the inequality of the social classes.* Chicago: The University of Chicago Press, 1938.

LaRossa, R. *Conflict and power in marriage.* Beverly Hills, Calif.: Sage, 1977.

Laslett, P. Societal development and aging. In R. Binstock and E. Shanas (Eds.), *Handbook of aging and the social sciences.* New York: Van Nostrand Reinhold, 1976.

Laufer, R., & Bengtson, V. L. Generations, aging, and social stratification: On the development of generational units. *Journal of Social Issues,* 1974, *30,* 181–206.

Lawton, M. P., & Kleban, M. H. The aged resident of the inner city. *Gerontologist,* 1971, *11,* 277–283.

Leggett, J. C. *Race, class, and political consciousness.* Cambridge: Schenkman, 1972.

Lehman, E. W. *Political society: A macrosociology of politics.* New York: Columbia University Press, 1977.

Lemert, E. M. Paranoia and the dynamics of exclusion. *Sociometry,* 1962, *25,* 2–20.

Lenski, G. E. *Power and privilege: A theory of social stratification.* New York: McGraw-Hill, 1966.

References 139

Lenski, G., & Lenski, J. *Human societies: An introduction to macrosociology.* New York: McGraw-Hill, 1978.

Levinson, D. J. The mid-life transition: A period in adult psychosocial development. *Psychiatry,* 1977, *40,* 99–112.

Levison, A. *The working-class majority.* New York: Penguin, 1975.

Lewytzkyj, B. Generations in conflict. *Problems of Communism,* 1967, *16,* 36–40.

Li, C. C., & Sacks, L. The derivation of joint distribution and correlation between relatives by the use of stochastic matrices. *Biometrics,* 1954, *10,* 347–460.

Lieberson, S. Generational differences among Blacks in the North. *American Journal of Sociology,* 1973, *79,* 550–565.

Lindblom, C. E. *Politics and markets.* New York: Basic Books, 1977.

Lipman, A. Prestige of the aged in Portugal: Realistic appraisal and ritualistic deference. *International Journal of Aging and Human Development,* 1970, *1,* 127–136.

Lockwood, D. The new working class. *European Journal of Sociology,* 1960, *1,* 248–259.

Lorenz, K. The enmity between generations and its ethological causes. *Psychoanalytic Review,* 1970, *57,* 334–377.

Lovald, K. A. Social life of the aged homeless man in skid row. *Gerontologist,* 1961, *1,* 30–33.

Lowenberg, P. A psycho-historical approach: The Nazi generation. From The psychohistorical origins of the Nazi Youth Cohort, *American Historical Review,* 1971, *76,* 1457–1502.

Lowenthal, M. F., & Robinson, B. Social networks and isolation. In R. Binstock and E. Shanas (Eds.), *Handbook of aging and the social sciences.* New York: Van Nostrand Reinhold, 1976.

Luckmann, T., & Berger, P. Social mobility and personal identity. *Archives Europeenes de Sociologie,* 1964, *5,* 331–344.

Lukes, S. *Individualism.* New York: Harper & Row, 1973.

Lutz, R. R. The generation as a social myth: The Viennese Academic Legion: Fathers and sons in the Vienna Revolution of 1848. *Journal of Central European Affairs,* 1962, *22,* 161–173.

MacIver, R. M. *Community: A sociological study.* London: Macmillan, 1927.

MacIver, R. M. *The ramparts we guard.* New York: Macmillan, 1950.

Maddox, G. L., & Wiley, J. Scope, concepts, and methods in the study of aging. In R. Binstock and E. Shanas (Eds.), *Handbook of aging and the social sciences.* New York: Van Nostrand Reinhold, 1976.

Maine, H. S. *Ancient law.* New York: Henry Holt, 1906.

Mandel, E. *Marxist economic theory.* London: Merlin Press, 1971.

Mannheim, K. The problem of generations. In Paul Kecskemeti (Ed.), *Essays on the sociology of knowledge.* London: Routledge & Kegan Paul, 1952.

Mannheim, K. *Ideology and utopia: An introduction to the sociology of knowledge.* New York: Harcourt Brace Jovanovich, 1955.

Marcuse, H. *One dimensional man: Studies in the ideology of advanced industrial society.* Boston: Beacon Press, 1964.

Mariolis, P. Interlocking directorates and control of corporations: The theory of bank control. *Social Science Quarterly,* 1975, *56,* 425–439.

Markson, E. W. A touch of class? A case study of geriatric screening process. *International Journal of Aging and Human Development,* 1974, *5,* 187–196.

Marshall, V. W. *Bernice Neugarten: Gerontologist in search of a theory.* Paper presented at the Annual Meetings of the Gerontological Society, New York, 1976.

Marshall, V. W. No exit: A symbolic interactionist perspective on aging. *International Journal of Aging and Human Development,* 1979, *9,* 345–358.

Martin, R. The concept of power: A critical defense. *British Journal of Sociology,* 1971, *22,* 240–257.

Mason, K. O., Mason, W., Winsborough, H. H., & Poole, W. K. Some methodological issues in the cohort analysis of archival data. *American Sociological Review,* 1973, *38,* 242–251.

Matthews, S. H. Old women and identity maintenance: Outwitting the grim reaper. *Urban Life,* 1975, *4,* 105–115.

Matthews, S. H. *Negotiation by default: The social definition of old widows.* Paper presented at the Society for the Study of Social Problems Meetings, Chicago, 1977.

McCall, G. J., & Simmons, J. L. *Identities and interactions.* New York: Free Press, 1966.

McClosky, H., & Schaar, J. H. Psychological dimensions of anomy. *American Sociological Review,* 1965, *30,* 14–40.

McCord, W., & McCord, A. *Power and equity.* New York: Praeger, 1977.

Meacher, M. *Taken for a ride.* London: Longman, 1972.

Meeker, B. F. Decisions and exchange. *American Sociological Review,* 1971, *36,* 485–495.

Mennell, S. *Sociological theory: Uses and unities.* London: Nelson, 1974.

Michelon, L. C. The new leisure class. *American Journal of Sociology,* 1954, *59,* 371–378.

Miller, J. Interlocking directorates flourish. *New York Times,* April 23, 1978.

Miller, S. M. The "new" working class. In A. B. Shostak and W. Gomberg (Eds.), *Blue-collar world.* Englewood Cliffs, N. J.: Prentice-Hall, 1965.

Mitchell, J. N. *Social exchange, dramaturgy, and ethnomethodology: Toward a paradigmatic synthesis.* New York: Elsevier North Holland, 1978.

Mitzman, A. *The iron cage: An historical interpretation of Max Weber.* New York: Knopf, 1970.

Mitzman, A. *Sociology and estrangement.* New York: Knopf, 1973.

Mizruchi, E. *Abeyance process and time: An exploratory approach to age and social structure.* Paper presented at the Working Conference on Time and Aging, Maxwell Policy Center on Aging, Casenovia, New York, 1977.

Moen, E. The reluctance of the elderly to accept help. *Social Problems,* 1978, *25,* 293–303.

Mommsen, W. J. *The age of bureaucracy.* Oxford: Basil Blackwell, 1974.

Moore, W. E. But some are more equal than others. *American Sociological Review,* 1963, *28,* 13–18.

Myerhoff, B. G. *Honor, anger, and autonomy in a senior citizen's center.* Paper presented at the Annual Meetings of the Gerontological Society, Louisville, 1975.

Nagel, J. D. A new look at the Soviet elite: A generational model of the Soviet system. *Journal of Political and Military Sociology,* 1975, *3,* 1–13.

Nelsen, E. N., & Nelsen, E. E. *"Passing" in the age stratification system.* Paper presented at the Annual Meetings of the American Sociological Association, New Orleans, 1972.

Neugarten, B. L. Continuities and discontinuities of psychological issues into adult life. *Human Development,* 1969, *12,* 121–130.

Neugarten, B. L. Age groups in American society and the rise of the young-old. In F. R. Eisele (Ed.), *Political consequences of aging.* Philadelphia: American Academy of Political and Social Sciences, 1974.

Neugarten, B. L., & Datan, N. D. Sociological perspectives on the life cycle. In P. Baltes and K. W. Schaie (Eds.), *Life-span developmental psychology: Personality and socialization.* New York: Academic Press, 1973.

Neugarten, B. L., & Hagestad, G. O. Age and the life course. In R. Binstock and E. Shanas (Eds.), *Handbook of aging and the social sciences.* New York: Van Nostrand Reinhold, 1976.

Neugarten, B. L., Havighurst, R. J., & Tobin, S. S. The measurement of life satisfaction. *Journal of Gerontology,* 1961, *16,* 134–143.

Newman, S. The conflict of generations in continental Europe. *Vital Speeches,* 1939, *5,* 623–628.

Ng, Wing-Cheung. *The dual labor-market theory: An evaluation of its status in the field of ethnic studies.* Paper presented at the Annual Meetings of the American Sociological Association, Chicago, 1977.

Nisbet, R. A. *The sociological tradition.* New York: Basic Books, 1966.

Nisbet, R. A. *Twilight of authority.* New York: Oxford, 1975.

Nuttall, R. L., & Fozard, J. L. Age, socio-economic status, and human abilities. *International Journal of Aging and Human Development,* 1970, *1,* 161–169.

O'Connor, J. *The fiscal crisis of the state.* New York: St. Martin's Press, 1973.

Ortega y Gasset, J. *Man and Crisis* (M. Adams, trans.). New York: Norton, 1958.

Otto, L. B., & Featherman, D. L. Social-structural and psychological antecedents of self-estrangement and powerlessness. *American Sociological Review,* 1975, *40,* 701–719.

Paillot, P. Criteria of independent (autonomous) life in old age. In J. M. A. Munnichs and W. J. A. Van den Heuvel (Eds.), *Dependency or interdependency in old age.* The Hague: Martinus Nijhoff, 1976.

Palmore, E. When can age, period, and cohort be separated? *Social Forces,* 1978, *57,* 282–295.

Palmore, E. B., & Manton, K. Modernization and status of the aged: International correlations. *Journal of Gerontology,* 1974, *29,* 205–210.

Palmore, E., & Whittington, F. Trends in the relative status of the aged. *Social Forces,* 1971, *50,* 84–91.

Pampel, F. C., & Choldin, H. M. Urban location and segregation of the aged: A block-level analysis. *Social Forces*, 1978, *56*, 1121–1139.

Parelius, A. P. Lifelong education and age stratification: Some unexpected relationships. *American Behavioral Scientist*, 1975, *19*, 206–223.

Parenti, M. *Power and the powerless*. New York: St. Martin's Press, 1978.

Parsons, T. *The structure of social action*. New York: McGraw-Hill, 1937.

Parsons, T. *The social system*. Glencoe, Ill.: Free Press, 1951.

Phillips, B. S. A role theory approach to adjustment in old age. *American Sociological Review*, 1957, *22*, 212–217.

Piore, M. J. The dual labor market: Theory and implications. In D. M. Gordon (Ed.), *Problems in political economy*. Lexington, Mass.: D. C. Heath, 1977.

Pollak, O. *Social adjustment in old age: A research planning report*. New York: Social Science Research Council, 1948.

Porter, J. *The vertical mosaic*. Toronto: University of Toronto Press, 1965.

Poulantzas, N. *Classes in contemporary capitalism* (trans., David Fernbach). Atlantic Highlands, N. J.: Humanities Press, 1975.

Pye, L. W. China: The politics of gerontocracy. In R. J. Samuels (Ed.), *Political generations and political development*. Lexington, Mass.: Lexington, 1977.

Ragan, P. K., & Dowd, J. J. The emerging political consciousness of the aged: A generational interpretation. *Journal of Social Issues*, 1974, *30*, 137–158.

Redfield, R. The folk society. *American Journal of Sociology*, 1947, *52*, 293–308.

Reich, M., Gordon, D. M., & Edwards, R. C. A theory of labor market segmentation. In D. M. Gordon (Ed.), *Problems in political economy*. Lexington, Mass.: D. C. Heath, 1977.

Reichard, S., Livson, F., & Peterson, P. *Aging and personality*. New York: Wiley, 1962.

Riesman, D., Glazer, N., & Denny, R. *The lonely crowd: A study of the changing American character*. New Haven: Yale University Press, 1950.

Riley, M. W. Social gerontology and the age stratification of society. *Gerontologist*, 1971, *11*, 79–82.

Riley, M. W. Aging and cohort succession: Interpretations and misinterpretations. *Public Opinion Quarterly*, 1973, *37*, 35–49.

Riley, M. W. The perspective of age stratification. *School Review*, 1974, *83*, 85–91.

Riley, M. W. Age strata in social systems. In R. Binstock and E. Shanas (Eds.), *Handbook of aging and the social sciences*. New York: Van Nostrand Reinhold, 1976.

Riley, M. W., Johnson, M., & Foner, A. *A sociology of stratification*, Volume 3 in *Aging and society*. New York: Basic Books, 1972.

Rintala, M. The problem of generations in Finnish communism. *American Slavic and East European Review*, 1958, *17*, 190–202.

Rintala, M. A generation in politics. *Review of Politics*, 1963, *25*, 509–522.

Rosdolsky, R. *The making of Marx's "Capital"* (trans., P. Burgess.). London: Pluto Press, 1977.

Rose, A. M. Group consciousness among the aging. In A. M. Rose and W. A. Peterson (Eds.), *Older people and their social world*. Philadelphia: F. A. Davis, 1965.

Rose, A. Class differences among the elderly: A research project. *Sociology and Social Research*, 1966, *50*, 356–360.

Rosenberg, G. S. Age, poverty, and isolation from friends in the urban working class. *Journal of Gerontology*, 1968, *24*, 533–538.

Rosenberg, G. S. *The worker grows old*. San Francisco: Jossey-Bass, 1970.

Rosenfeld, J. P. *Bequests from resident to resident: Patterns of inheritance in a retirement community*. Paper presented at the Annual Meetings of the American Sociological Association, San Francisco, 1978.

Rosenfelt, R. M. The elderly mystique. *Journal of Social Issues*, 1965, *21*, 37–43.

Rosenmayr, L. *Elements of an assimilation-yield theory: An exchange model for gerosociology*. Paper presented at the 8th World Congress of Sociology, Toronto, 1974.

Rosenmayr, L. The family—a source of hope for the elderly. In E. Shanas and M. B. Sussman (Eds.), *Family bureaucracy and the elderly*. Durham, N. C.: Duke University Press, 1977.

Rosenmayr, L., & Eder, A. *Family and future: Reflections and data on intergenerational relations and social change*. Paper presented at the 11th International Congress of Gerontology, Tokyo, 1978.

Rosow, I. *Social integration of the aged*. New York: Free Press. 1967.

Rosow, I. *Socialization to old age*. Berkeley: University of California, 1974.

References

Rosow, I. Status and role change through the life span. In R. Binstock and E. Shanas (Eds.), *Handbook of aging and the social sciences*. New York: Van Nostrand Reinhold, 1976.

Ross, J. K. *Old people, new lives*. Chicago: University of Chicago Press, 1977.

Rothman, R. A. *Inequality and stratification in the United States*. Englewood Cliffs, N. J.: Prentice-Hall, 1978.

Rowles, G. D. *Prisoners of space? Exploring the geographical experience of older people*. Boulder: Westview Press, 1978.

Rowntree, J., & Rowntree, M. Youth as a class. *International Socialist Journal*, 1968, *25*, 25–58.

Russell, B. The pros and cons of reaching ninety. *The autobiography of Bertrand Russell, 1944–1969*. New York: Simon & Schuster, 1969.

Ryder, N. The cohort as a concept in the study of social change. *American Sociological Review*, 1965, *30*, 843–861.

Ryder, N. Notes on the concept of a population. In M. Riley, M. Johnson, and A. Foner (Eds.), *Aging and society*. New York: Russell Sage, 1972.

Schroyer, T. *The critique of domination*. New York: Braziller, 1973.

Scott, M., & Lyman, S. Accounts. *American Sociological Review*, 1968, *33*, 46–62.

Seguin, M. Opportunity for peer socialization in a retirement community. *Gerontologist*, 1973, *13*, 208–214.

Seider, J. S. American big business ideology: A content analysis of executive speeches. *American Sociological Review*, 1974, *39*, 802–815.

Shanan, J., & Weihl, H. Forces and autonomous detachment, their relationships to coping style and independence in later adulthood. In J. M. A. Munnichs and V. J. A. Van den Heuvel (Eds.), *Dependency or interdependency in old age*. The Hague: Martinus Nijhoff, 1976.

Snanas, E. Family help patterns and social class in three countries. *Journal of Marriage and the Family*, 1967, *29*, 257–266.

Shanas, E., & Hauser, P. M. Zero population growth and the family life of old people. *Journal of Social Issues*, 1974, *30*, 79–92.

Shanas, E., Townsend, P., Wedderburn, D., Friis, H., Milhog, P., & Stehouwer, J. *Older people in three industrial societies*. New York: Atherton, 1968.

Sheehan, T. Senior esteem as a factor of socioeconomic complexity. *Gerontologist*, 1976, *16*, 433–440.

Sheleff, L. S. Beyond the Oedipus complex: A perspective on the myth and reality of generational conflict. *Theory and Society*, 1976, *3*, 1–44.

Sheppard, H. L. Work and retirement. In R. Binstock and E. Shanas (Eds.), *Handbook of aging and the social sciences*. New York: Van Nostrand Reinhold, 1976.

Shils, E. *Center and periphery: Essays in macrosociology*. Chicago: University of Chicago Press, 1975.

Sidgwick, H. *The methods of ethics*. New York: Dover, 1966.

Simirenko, A. Karl Mannheim's generational analysis and acculturation. *British Journal of Sociology*, 1966, *17*, 292–299.

Simmons, L. W. *The role of the aged in primitive society*. New Haven: Yale University Press, 1945.

Simpson, A. P. Social class correlates of old age. *Sociology and Social Research*, 1961, *45*, 131–139.

Slater, P. Cross-cultural views of the aged. In R. Kastenbaum (Ed.), *New thoughts on old age*. New York: Springer, 1964.

Slater, P. *Origin and significance of the Frankfurt School*. London: Routledge & Kegan Paul, 1977.

Smelser, N. J. *A theory of collective behavior*. New York: Free Press, 1963.

Smith, A. *The wealth of nations*. New York: Modern Library, 1937.

Smith, D. H., & Inkeles, A. The O M scale: A comparative socio-psychological measure of individual modernity. *Sociometry*, 1966, *12*, 353–377.

Smith, D. S. Old age and the "Great Transformation": A New England case study. In S. Spicker, K. Woodward, and D. D. van Tassel (Eds.), *Aging and the elderly*. Atlantic Highlands, N. J.: Humanities Press, 1978.

Sniderman, P., & Citrin, J. Psychological sources of political beliefs: Self-esteem and isolationist attitudes. *American Political Science Review*, 1971, *65*, 401–417.

References 143

Solem, E. Dependency—due to lack of individual or environmental resources? In J. M. A. Munnichs and V. J. A. Van den Heuvel (Eds.), *Dependency or interdependency in old age.* The Hague: Martinus Nijhoff, 1976.

Sonquist, J., & Koenig, T. Interlocking directorates in the top United States corporations: A graph theory approach. *Insurgent Sociologist*, 1975, *5*, 196–229.

Soref, M. Social class and a division of labor within the corporate elite: A note on class, interlocking, and executive committee membership of directors of United States firms. *The Sociological Quarterly*, 1976, *17*, 360–368.

Sorokin, P. *Social and cultural dynamics.* Boston: Porter Sargent, 1957.

Speier, H. The social determination of ideas. *Social Research*, May, 1938.

Speier, H. *Social order and the risks of war.* Cambridge: M.I.T. Press, 1952.

Spitzer, A. B. The historical problem of generations. *American Historical Review*, 1973, *78*, 1353–1385.

Stannard, D. E. Growing up and growing old: Dilemmas of aging in bureaucratic America. In S. Spicker, K. Woodward, D. D. van Tassel (Eds.), *Aging and the elderly.* Atlantic Highlands, N. J.: Humanities Press, 1978.

Stearns, P. N. *Old age in industrial society: The case of France.* New York: Holmes & Meiers, 1976.

Stephens, J. Carnies and Marks: The sociology of elderly street peddlers. *Sociological Symposium*, 1974, *11*, 25–41.

Stephens, J. Society of the alone: Freedom, privacy, and utilitarianism as dominant norms in the SRO. *Journal of Gerontology*, 1975, *30*, 230–235.

Stinchcombe, A. L. Some empirical consequences of the Davis-Moore theory of stratification. *American Sociological Review*, 1963, *28*, 387–394.

Stinchcombe, A. L. Organized dependency relations and social stratification. In E. O. Laumann, P. Siegel, and R. W. Hodge (Eds.), *The logic of social hierarchies.* Chicago: Markham, 1970.

Stokes, R., & Hewitt, J. P. Aligning actions. *American Sociological Review*, 1976, *41*, 838–849.

Stolte, J. F., & Emerson, R. M. Structural inequality: Position and power in network structures. In R. L. Hamblin and J. H. Kunkel (Eds.), *Behavioral theory in sociology.* New Brunswick, N. J.: Transaction, 1977.

Stolzenberg, R. M. Education, occupation, and wage differences between White and Black men. *American Journal of Sociology*, 1975, *81*, 299–323. (a)

Stolzenberg, R. M. Occupations, labor markets, and the process of wage attainment. *American Sociological Review*, 1975, *40*, 645–665. (b)

Streib, G. F. Are the aged a minority group? In A. W. Gouldner and S. M. Miller (Eds.), *Applied sociology.* Glencoe, Ill.: Free Press, 1965.

Streib, G. F. Disengagement theory in sociocultural perspective. *International Journal of Psychiatry*, 1968, *6*, 69–76.

Streib, G. F. Social stratification and aging. In R. Binstock and E. Shanas (Eds.), *Handbook of aging and the social sciences.* New York: Van Nostrand Reinhold, 1976.

Streib, G. F., & Streib, R. B. Communes and the aging: Utopian dream and gerontological reality. *American Behavior Science*, 1975, *19*, 176–189.

Streib, G. F., & Streib, R. B. *Retired persons and their contributions: Exchange theory.* Paper presented at the 11th International Congress of Gerontology, Tokyo, 1978.

Sussman, M. B. Relationships of adult children with their parents in the United States. In E. Shanas and G. Streib (Eds.), *Social structure and the family: Generational relations.* Englewood Cliffs, N. J.: Prentice-Hall, 1965.

Sussman, M. B. The family life of old people. In R. Binstock and E. Shanas (Eds.), *Handbook of aging and the social sciences.* New York: Van Nostrand Reinhold, 1976.

Sussman, M. B. Family, bureaucracy, and the elderly individual: An organizational linkage perspective. In E. Shanas and M. Sussman (Eds.), *Family, bureaucracy, and the elderly.* Durham, N. C.: Duke University Press, 1977.

Suttles, G. D., & Street, D. Aid to the poor and social exchange. In E. O. Laumann, P. M. Siegel, and R. W. Hodge (Eds.), *The logic of social hierarchies.* Chicago: Markham, 1970.

Thibaut, J. W., & Kelley, H. H. *The social psychology of groups.* New York: Wiley, 1959.

Tibbles, L. Medical and legal aspects of competency as affected by old age. In S. Spicker, K. Woodward, and D. D. van Tassel (Eds.), *Aging and the elderly.* Atlantic Highlands, N. J.: Humanities Press, 1978.

Tindale, J. A., & Marshall, V. W. *Generational conflict theory in gerontology.* Paper presented at the Annual Meetings of the Canadian Association on Gerontology, Edmonton, 1978.

Tiryakian, E. A. The time perspectives of modernity. *Society and Leisure,* 1978, *1,* 125–156.

Tissue, T. Downward mobility in old age. *Social Problems,* 1970, *18,* 67–77.

Tissue, T. Old age, poverty, and the central city. *Aging and Human Development,* 1971, *2,* 235–248.

Tönnies, F. *Community and society* (C. A. Loomis, Ed. and trans.). East Lansing, Mich.: Michigan State University Press, 1957.

Torrance, E. P. Some consequences of power differences on decision making in permanent and temporary three-man groups. In A. P. Hare, E. F. Borgatta, and R. F. Bales (Eds.), *Small Groups.* New York: Knopf, 1955.

Touraine, A. *The post-industrial society.* New York: Random House, 1971.

Treas, J. *Socialist organization and economic development in China: Latent consequences for the aged.* Paper presented at the Annual Meetings of the Gerontological Society, Dallas, 1978.

Trela, J. E. Social class and political involvement in age-graded and non-age-graded associations. *International Journal of Aging and Human Development,* 1977–78, *8,* 301–310.

Treves, R. Fascism and the problem of generations. *Quaderni di Sociologia,* 1964, *13,* 119–146.

Trivers, R. L. The evolution of reciprocal altruism. *Quarterly Review of Biology, 1971, 46,* 35–57.

Trivers, R. L. Parent-offspring conflict. *American Zoologist,* 1974, *14,* 249–264.

Tumin, M. Some principles of stratification: A critical analysis. *American Sociological Review,* 1953, *18,* 387–394.

Tumin, M. On inequality. *American Sociological Review,* 1963, *28,* 19–26.

Useem, M. The inner group of the American capitalist class. *Social Problems,* 1978, *25,* 225–240.

van den Berghe, P. Dialectic and functionalism: Toward a theoretical synthesis. *American Sociological Review,* 1963, *28,* 695–705.

van den Berghe, P. L. *Age and sex in human societies: A biosocial perspective.* Belmont, Calif.: Wadsworth, 1973.

van den Heuvel, W. The meaning of dependency. In J. M. A. Munnichs and W. van den Heuvel (Eds.), *Dependency or interdependency in old age.* The Hague: Martinus Nijhoff, 1976.

Veblen, T. *The vested interests and the comman man.* New York: Viking, 1946 (1919).

Ward, R. Aging group consciousness: Implications in an older sample. *Sociology and Social Research,* 1977, *61,* 496–519.

Waring, J. M. Social replenishment and social change: The problem of disordered cohort flow. *American Behavioral Scientist,* 1975, *19,* 237–256.

Wattenberg, B. J. *The real America* (rev. ed.). New York: Capricorn, 1976.

Weber, M. *The theory of social and economic organization* (A. M. Henderson and T. Parsons, trans.). New York: Oxford University Press, 1947.

Weber, M. *Economy and society: An outline of interpretive sociology.* (G. Roth and C. Wittich, Eds.). New York: Bedminster Press, 1968.

Webster, M. Jr., & Driskell, J. E., Jr. Status generalization. *American Sociological Review,* 1978, *43,* 220–236.

Wershow, H. J. Reality orientation for gerontologists: Some thoughts about senility. *The Gerontologists,* 1977, *17,* 297–302.

Wheeler, R. F. German labor and the comintern: A problem of generations. *Journal of Social History,* 1974, *7,* 304–321.

Wilensky, H. L. *The welfare state and equality.* Berkeley: University of California Press, 1975.

Willmuth, S. *Mass society, social organization, and democracy.* New York: Philosophical Library, 1976.

Wilson, E. O. *Sociobiology: The new synthesis.* Cambridge: Harvard University Press, 1975.

Wilson, E. O. *On human nature.* Cambridge: Harvard University Press, 1978.

Winch, R. F., & Greer, S. A. Urbanism, ethnicity, and extended families. *Marriage and Family Living,* 1968, *30,* 40–45.

Wittermans, T., & Krauss, I. Structural marginality and social worth. *Sociology and Social Research,* 1964, *48,* 348–360.

Wright, E. O. Class boundaries in advanced capitalism. *New Left Review,* 1976, *98,* 3–42.

Wright, E. O. Race, class, and income inequality. *American Journal of Sociology,* 1978, *83,* 1368–1397.

References　　　　　　　　　　　　　　　　　　　　　　　　　　　*145*

Wright, E. O., & Perrone, L. Marxist class categories and income inequality. *American Sociological Review*, 1977, *42*, 32–55.

Wrong, D. H. Social inequality without social stratification. *Canadian Review of Sociology and Anthropology*, 1964, *1*, 5–16.

Wuthnow, R. Recent patterns and secularization: A problem of generations. *American Sociological Review*, 1976, *41*, 850–867.

Zajonc, R. B. Attitudinal effects of mere exposure. *Journal of Personality and Social Psychology*, Monograph Supplement, 1968, *9*, 1–127.

Zeitlin, I. M. *Rethinking sociology: A critique of contemporary theory*. Englewood Cliffs, N. J.: Prentice-Hall, 1973.

Zeitlin, M. *Revolutionary politics and the Cuban working class*. Princeton, N. J.: Princeton University Press, 1967.

Zeitlin, M. *Revolutionary politics and the Cuban working class*. Princeton, N. J.: Princeton University Press, 1970.

Zeitlin, M. Corporate ownership and control: The large corporation and the capitalist class. *American Journal of Sociology*, 1974, *79*, 1073–1119.

Zimmerman, C. C. *The changing community*. New York: Harper & Bros., 1938.

Name Index

Subject Index